Spenser and the System of Courtly Love

By

Earle B. Fowler, B.A., Ph.D.

PHAETON PRESS
NEW YORK
1968

Originally Published 1934
Reprinted 1968

PREFACE

Chapters II and III of this study were originally a part of an unpublished section of a monograph on *Spenser and the Courts of Love* (Menasha, 1921), which was undertaken some years ago as a doctoral dissertation at the University of Chicago. The remaining chapters have been written at intervals since that time.

E. B. F.

University of Louisville

Library of Congress Catalog Card Number 67-30903

Published by Phaeton Press, Inc.

CONTENTS

Spenser and the System of Courtly Love

I

INTRODUCTION:
THE SYSTEM OF COURTLY LOVE

The story of the origin and development of' the courtly
love system has been told so often that it seems superfluous to
repeat it.[1] Yet for the sake of the general reader it is necessary
to sketch it again as a background for the study of the courtly
conventions appearing in Spenser. The system began as a code
of manners, which eventually crystallized into a literary tradition. It was started by the troubadour poets of Provence about
the middle of the twelfth century and was promoted by Eleanor
of Aquitaine, who became Queen of France, and by her
daughter, Marie de Champagne. Marie encouraged the work
of the troubadours, one of whom, Bernart de Ventadorn (c.
1140–1195), is reputed to have been the lover of the countess.
These poets were influenced by Ovid's *Ars Amatoria* and
Remedia Amoris.[2] Ovid regarded love-making as an art, and
he elaborated a set of rules by which a lover might win and
keep a mistress. In Provencal poetry, then, love is regarded as
a warfare and the God of Love as a warrior, inconstant but
irresistible. Love increases the valiance and nobility of the
lover. It brings, paradoxically, both joy and woe, happiness and
melancholy. It causes dreams, doubts, fears, timidity, jealousy,
and mental anguish—especially in absence. The lover regards
himself as a willing slave—driven by love to despair or to
madness. He suffers burning desire—the flames of love—
extremes of heat and cold, loss of sleep, loss of speech, and
other serious ailments which usually threaten to end fatally.

---

[1] In addition to the pioneer work of Gaston Paris and other scholars, the following
more or less general accounts of the system may be cited:
    Lee, Vernon, *Euphorion*, Boston, 1884, 2 vols. (Vol. II, Chapter on
    "Mediaeval Love"); Mott, L. F., *The System of Courtly Love*, Bos-
    ton, 1896; Neilson, W. A., *The Origins and Sources of the Court of
    Love*, Boston, 1899; Dodd, W. G., *Courtly Love in Chaucer and Gower*,
    Boston and London, 1913.

[2] Schrötter, W., *Ovid und die Troubadours*, Halle, 1908.

In the presence of the beloved the lover sighs, sheds tears, trembles, and turns pale.

Quasi-judicial courts of love were held at Marie's court. One of the most important decisions rendered declared love and marriage incompatible. Andreas Capellanus codified the rules of "lady's service" and set forth the statutes of love in his book *De Amore*. According to these laws the *vilain* is excluded from love-making. Absolute loyalty, obedience, vassalage, and secrecy are required of the lover. He must be willing to suffer dishonor for his lady. He must believe no evil of her and must defend her honor. He must be clean and neat, joyful and merry. He must protest undying affection, complain of cruelty, and appeal to the lady's pity. Modesty in his relations with the lady is enjoined, and the pleasure of the beloved must not be exceeded. The lady must grant favors sparingly. Meddlers are warned against intrusion, lying, slander, and tale-bearing.

The organization of mediaeval society fostered the system. In theory this love was frankly sensual and adulterous. Marriage was a matter of convenience or of state. The lady of the castle was high-born, proud, and lovely—one woman among a throng of handsome courtiers eager to worship at her shrine. In such a situation love absorbed and overshadowed all interests, was never satisfied, and was pursued with religious zeal. It was part of a man's knighthood. Many of the troubadours— Count William IX of Poitou, for example—were lords.

At the court of Marie dwelt also the greatest of the French mediaeval romancers—Chrétien de Troyes (wrote 1160–1180). To him belongs the credit for grafting the courtly system on the Arthurian romances. With keen psychological subtlety Chrétien adds a few conceits of his own, the most famous being that the lover is wounded by the dart of Love, which passes through the eyes of the lover and thus reaches the heart without leaving an external wound. Although Chrétien applied the courtly system to the romances, he does not seem to have accepted personally the fundamental tenet of the system that love and marriage are incompatible. On the contrary, in all his romances save one—*Erec, Cligés, Yvain*—he upholds the idea of love in marriage; *amie* and *femme* are one. This one exception is the *Lancelot,* which was written to illustrate the law of absolute obedience of the knight to his lady. Why the change in the *Lancelot?* The answer is the Countess Marie, who, as Chrétien is careful to tell us, furnished the poet both subject and method of treatment. In a recent study of this romance Professors Cross and Nitze have shown that the framework of the abduction stories was probably derived from Celtic fairy lore and that there is nothing in the treatment of the love motive inconsistent with such a source. "In other words, both Arthur and Guenevere are eminently fitted by ancestry for husband and wife under the system of Courtly Love as elucidated below (p. 95). Whoever first conceived the idea of making a Celtic tale such as the Tochmar Étaine the vehicle of courtly psychology was little short of a genius."[3] Yet *l'amour courtois* in the *Lancelot* "owes its distinctive mark to the influence of the troubadours."[4] There alone is developed the idea of *amis entiers,* though it remained for Marie to weld the idea into a system.

In the first half of the thirteenth century the love doctrines of the romances were incorporated in the *Romance of the Rose* (c. 1237) and in the innumerable imitations of this work which flooded the Middle Ages with love allegories for almost three centuries.

About the same time, however, the art instinct among the Tuscan towns—already alive in painting and architecture—began to crave utterance in song. The Tuscan singers were influenced by the Provencal and Sicilian poets, but in a different social setting among the rising burghers and with equality of the sexes recognized they injected a new note which eventually wrought a fundamental change in the whole philosophy of love. In the troubadour poetry and in the early romances love ended in possession, but here love—become ideal and spiritual—renounced possession and ended in the poetic

[3] *Lancelot and Guenevere,* Chicago, 1930, p. 60.
[4] *Op. cit.,* p. 96.

tribute. Adulterous love may have continued as a social fact, but it was not recognized in the poetry of the *dolce stil nuovo*. The ideal love celebrated by Guinicelli, Cavalcante, and Dante was premonitory of the rising tide of Platonic philosophy which came in with the revival of classical learning.

In the *Symposium* Plato binds love in indissoluble bonds with beauty and virtue. Thus he defines love as the desire for the everlasting possession of the Good. Love is also of the beautiful and is defined by the Neo-Platonists as a certain coveting of beauty. According to Prof. R. V. Merrill[5], the Florentine Academy under the leadership of Ficino had interpreted Plato in the light of Plotinus' teaching, but Cardinal Bembo led a reaction from Ficino's Neo-Platonism to true Platonism in Renaissance amatory theory and was supported by Castiglione, "whose *Cortegiano* translated into terms of courtly behaviour the principles which Bembo had derived from Plato."[6] In the meantime the poets of the *dolce stil nuovo,* under the influence of St. Thomas' teaching about divine love, had supplied a philosophy for the *amour courtois*. This Petrarch took over, though he still had his basis in the courtly system and looked in vain for fulfillment of earthly love; whereas, Bembo looked to the idea of Beauty beyond earthly embodiment. Hence, according to the latter, the lover and lady march together towards virtue.

The Platonic conception of love and beauty did not contemplate love between the sexes. This limited application of the theory was due to Renaissance influence. Thus Renaissance Platonism starts with beauty in woman at the lowest rung of the Ladder of Love and mounts by successive stages to the concept of abstract Beauty in God. On the other hand, pure courtly love begins with beauty in woman and ends there. In theory the systems were still distinct, but the affinity of Christian and Platonic doctrine encouraged the fusion of the worship of the Virgin with the Platonic love philosophy to form the

---

[5] *The Platonism of Joachim du Bellay,* University of Chicago, Diss., 1923.
[6] *Op. cit.,* p. 4.

Renaissance religion of beauty in woman. This ideal passed into France and then into England side by side with the Petrarchan courtly tradition embodied in the sonnets to Laura. In France the lyrists of the Pléiade apparently swung from Petrarchism to Platonism and back again, or, to speak more accurately, they adopted the framework of the courtly system but idealized the love philosophy by an injection of Platonic doctrine.

Finally, by way of completing the background for the study of the courtly conventions in Spenser, let us summarize the course of the tradition in the Elizabethan age. An exhaustive study of this subject was made a number of years ago by Dr. Percy W. Long in his unpublished Harvard dissertation on *Elizabethan Courtly Love.* There is space here for only a brief summary of important generalizations from this study. The courtier is obligated to love by virtue of his station, and, being in love, must write of it. An exception to the rule excluding the *vilain* is the pastoral convention. In general, the rules of obedience, constancy, and secrecy were retained. The pains of lovers were elaborated in the traditional manner. The basic opposition of Ovidian and Platonic doctrines continued. The lady's formal attitude of chaste austerity was encouraged by the Queen, who was always compared to Diana rather than to Venus. Hence, while courtly love in theory remained sensual, actually it had to be more and more refined, courteous, and noble. Though married ladies might receive the homage of the courtly poet, unmarried couples were now also admitted to love.

On the whole, though Dr. Long does not distinctly emphasize the point, there is reason to believe that two schools of courtly poets existed in the Elizabethan Age, representing respectively the Ovidian and the Neo-Platonic traditions. To which of these schools did Spenser belong? To answer this and other related questions we turn now to a more detailed study of the influence of the courtly system on Spenser.

II

THE COURTLY SYSTEM IN SPENSER: SYMPTOMS
AND EFFECTS OF LOVE

Of the beneficent effects of love the courtly system recognizes three as of special value: increase of knightly prowess, growth in nobility of character (*pris* or *pros*), and enhancement of personal happiness. These will be taken up in order.

Love increases the personal valor and prowess of the lover. In Chrétien's *Lancelot,* as the hero struggles with his adversary, he keeps his eye on the Queen who had kindled in him the flame which compels his gaze:

> Et cele flame si ardant
> Vers Meleagant le feisoit
> Que par tot la ou li pleisoit
> Le pooit mener et chacier.
> (vv. 3770–3773.)[1]

Spenser says that Cupid with his dart at Prince Arthur

> so cunningly didst rove
> That glorious fire it kindled in his hart,

making him wander through the world and suffer all manner of ill for the sake of his love (*F. Q.,* Invocation, 2–3).

Love is the source of all martial glory.[2] Spenser says that those who condemn love do so in ignorance:

---

[1] As Prof. Nitze points out (*Mod. Phil.*, XI, 1914, pp. 449 and 456), this motive is found even earlier than Chrétien in Geoffrey of Monmouth and Wace. Cf. also Ovid, *Epist.*, XVII, 93–94.

[2] D'amors vient joie et honor ausiment,
Ne nuls ne puet avoir entierement
Prix ne valor, s'amor ne le jostise.
(Bédier, *De Nicolao Museto,* p. 25.)

Chaucer says that, save Hector, Troilus was the most feared warrior in Troy:
And this encrees of hardinesse and might
Cam him of love, his ladies thank to winne,
That altered his spirit so with-inne.
(*Troilus and Criseyde,* III, 1776–1778.)

For it of honor and all vertue is
The roote, and brings forth glorious flowres of fame,
That crowne true lovers with immortall blis,
The meed of them that love, and do not live amisse.

Which who so list looke backe to former ages,
And call to count the things that then were donne,
Shall find, that all the workes of those wise sages,
And brave exploits which great heroes wonne,
In love were either ended or begunne.
(*F. Q.*, IV, Introd., 2–3.)

For love is

that sweete fit that doth true beautie love,
And chooseth Vertue for his dearest dame,
Whence spring all noble deedes and never dying fame.
(*F. Q.*, III, iii, 1.)

It stirs up

th' heroes high intents,
Which the late world admyres for wondrous moniments.
(*F. Q.*, III, iii, 2.)

Britomart spurs to meet her foe because

Love and despight attonce her courage kindled hath.
(*F. Q.*, III, iv, 12.)[3]

In the courtly romances the lady herself becomes the direct source of valor and prowess.[4] Wrapped in the toils of the dragon Error, the Redcross Knight is powerless to move till roused by the voice of Una:

That when he heard, in great perplexitie,
His gall did grate for griefe and high disdaine;
And knitting all his force, got one hand free,
Wherewith he grypt her gorge with so great paine,
That soone to loose her wicked bands did
her constraine (*F. Q.*, I, i, 19).

[3] In *Der Kittel* Venus tells the lover what love can do for him:
Sie tuot dich turneren stechen,
Sie tuot dich manig sper brechen.
(*Bib. d. Lit. Ver. in Stuttgart*, vol. XXI, 1850, p. 64.)

[4] In the combat for the sparrow-hawk in Chrétien's *Erec*, as the knights pause for breath,
Erec regarde vers s'amie
Qui por lui mout doucement prie.
Tot maintenant qu'il l'a veüe
Li est mout granz force creüe.
Por s'amor et por sa biauté
A reprise mout grant fierté (vv. 911–916).
Cf. *F. Q.*, I, v, 12.

The lady is the source of strength even when absent from the scene of combat.[5]   In such case it is the image of her beauty that incites to battle.   Influenced by this the lover always bethinks him

> What he may do, her favour to obtaine;
> What brave exploit, what perill hardly wrought,
> What puissant conquest, what adventurous paine,
> May please her best, and grace unto him gaine:
> He dreads no danger, nor misfortune feares;
> His faith, his fortune in his breast he beares.
> (*Hymne in Honour of Love*, vv. 219–224.)

Love leads the poet to higher achievement.[6]   In the October eclogue of the *Shepheardes Calender* Piers says that Colin's love for Rosalind, so far from being a bar to higher poetic flight, really exalts him:

> Such immortall mirrhor as he doth admire
> Would rayse ones mynd above the starry skie,
> And cause a caytive corage to aspire;
> For lofty love doth loath a lowly eye.
> (vv. 93–96.)

In the invocation to the *Faerie Queene* Spenser prays to his sovereign:

> Shed thy faire beames into my feeble eyne,
> And raise my thoughts, too humble and too vile,
> To think of that true glorious type of thine,
> The argument of mine afflicted stile.[7]

In *Amoretti* 3 he says that the beauty of his lady has kindled heavenly fire in his frail spirit, "by her from basenesse raysed," so that he can no longer endure to view base thing.

---

[5] When about to try the enchantment of the Forbidden Chamber, Amadis of Gaul prays to his absent Lady Oriana, from whom, he says, "onely proceedeth all the strength and courage that ever I had."   He enters and tremendous blows begin to light upon him. "Yet his courage so much increased with the onely remembrance of Oriana that there were never any knight before which could come neere him."
(*Amadis de Gaule*, London, 1619, Book II, ch. 2, p. 11.)

[6] The troubadour Peire Vidal says that he owes his knowledge of the poetic art to his lady:

> e tot quan fauc d'avinen
> ai del seu bel cors plazen,
> neis quan de bon cor consire.
> (Appel, *Prov. Chrest.*, p. 65, No. 23, vv. 22–28.)

[7] The use of Platonic terms in this and other passages suggests the close connection between the courtly and the Platonic systems at this point.

Love is the spur to all honorable, generous conduct:

> For love does alwaies bring forth bounteous deeds,
> And in each gentle hart desire of honor breeds.
> (*F. Q.*, III, i, 49.)[8]

In the garden of the Temple of Venus Scudamour saw a band of congenial spirits whose love, grounded on "chaste vertue,"

> in their spirits kindling zealous fire,
> Brave thoughts and noble deedes did evermore aspire.
> (*F. Q.*, IV, x, 26.)

In Spenser this attribute of courtly love blends with Neo-Platonic thought and finally disappears in a haze of mysticism.[9]

From love springs all the lover's happiness and joy. Says William IX of Poitou:

> toty lo ioys del mon es nostre,
> dompna, s'amduy nos amam.[10]

In *Amoretti* 8 the poet finds such joy in the eyes of his lady:

> No eies, but joyes, in which al powers conspire,
> That to the world naught else be counted deare.

As the lover's long-tossed bark descries the shore, he exclaims:

> All paines are nothing in respect of this,
> All sorrowes short that gaine eternall blisse.
> (*Amoretti* 63.)

Possessed of his lady's heart and hand the Redcross Knight holds himself "thrise happy," and his heart melts in manifold

---

[8] Per lui gli amanti cognosciono onore;
In adornezze e in piacer li mantene,
E poi largisce la corona e il manto.
(*Poeti del primo secolo*, II, p. 407.)

[9] See *An Hymne in Honour of Love*, vv. 190–196 and *An Hymne of Heavenly Love*, vv. 1–4.
The highest compliment the mediaeval mind could pay to the power of love was that it could transform a *vilain* into a courtier. See Mätzner, *Altfr. Lieder*, pp. 60 and 255; Andreas Capellanus, *De Amore*, ed. by Trojel, p. 10; Huon de Méry, *Le Tornoiement de l'Antéchrist*, ed. by Tarbé, Reims, 1851, p. 53; and Bédier, *De Nicolao Museto*, p. 25. Strangely enough I have not seen in Spenser a clear-cut example of this commonplace.

[10] Appel, *Prov. Chrest.*, p. 52. Cf. *ibid.*, p. 58; Mätzner, *Altfr. Lieder*, p. 14, vv. 14–16 and note, pp. 152–153; and *Der Kittel in Bibl. d. Lit. Ver. in Stuttgart*, vol. XXI, 1850, p. 64.

pleasures when he looks upon her (*F. Q.*, I, xii, 40).[11]   When
Britomart heard the name Artegall,

> Her hart did leape, and all her hartstringes tremble,
> For sudden joy (*F. Q.*, IV, vi, 29).

Later Glauce begged her to grant the knight her grace:

> Thereat full inly blushed Britomart;
> But Artegall, close smyling, joy'd in secret hart.
> (*F. Q.*, IV, vi, 32.)

The courtesy of Sir Calidore in the mind of Pastorella the seeds

> Of perfect love did sow, that last forth brought
> The fruite of joy and blisse, though long time dearely
>   bought (*F. Q.*, VI, ix, 45).

In his prayer to the goddess in the Temple of Venus the lover
says:

> Thou art the root of all that joyous is,
> Great god of men and women, queene of th' ayre,
> Mother of laughter, and welspring of blisse,
> O graunt that of my love at last I may not misse.
> (*F. Q.*, IV, x, 47.)

In the original conclusion of Book III of the *Faerie Queene*
Scudamour and Amoretta, united by Britomart, rushed into
each other's arms, and Amoretta, overcome

> Of huge affection, did in pleasure melt,
> And in sweete ravishment pourd out her spright:
> No word they spake, nor earthly thing they felt,
> But like two senceles stocks in long embracement dwelt.[12]

The lover is ravished with joy by the slightest token of
his lady's affection. It may be merely an eye-glance, as when
the false Florimell plays the coquette with Blandamour—

> Sometimes him blessing with a light eye-glance,
> And coy lookes tempring with loose dalliance;
> Sometimes estranging him in sterner wise;

---

[11] Cf. the Knight's "swimming in that sea of blisfull joy" in the next stanza.
[12] *F. Q.*, III, xii, 45 (1590 edition), *Works*, ed. by Dodge, p. 768.

> That, having cast him in a foolish trance,
> He seemed brought to bed in Paradise,
> And prov'd himselfe most foole in what he seem'd
>   most wise (*F. Q.*, IV, ii, 9).

In *Amoretti* 39 the poet is melted with gladness by his lady's smile:

> Whylest rapt with joy resembling heavenly madnes,
> My soule was ravisht quite, as in a traunce,
> And feeling thence no more her sorrowes sadnesse,
> Fed on the fulnesse of that chearefull glaunce.[13]

If the lady should yield so far as to grant the lover her grace, then indeed has he attained the *summum bonum*:

> And if by all these perils and these paynes
> He may but purchase lyking in her eye,
> What heavens of joy then to himselfe he faynes!
>   (*Hymne in Honour of Love*, vv. 238–240.)

A second group of courtly commonplaces is concerned with the mental and temperamental symptoms and effects of love. Oftener than otherwise these effects are quite the reverse of joyful. The lover becomes pensive, moody, and melancholy.[14] In the January eclogue of the *Shepheardes Calender* Colin Clout gives vent to his hopeless love for Rosalind, and then, as night draws on,

> the pensife boy, halfe in despight,
> Arose, and homeward drove his sonned sheepe,
> Whose hanging heads did seeme his carefull case to weepe.
>   (vv. 76–78.)

The lady is sometimes similarly affected.[15] Britomart sees in Merlin's magic mirror the image of Artegall and loves it:

---

[13] Cf. Petrarch, Sonetto CCLVIII: "Vive faville uscian."

[14] For an interesting discussion of lovers' *melancolia*—with its accompanying pathological symptoms—from the point of view of mediaeval medicine, see Lowes, "The Loveres Maladye Hereos," *Mod. Phil.*, vol. 11, pp. 491 ff.

[15] In Chrétien's *Cligés* Alexander and his Greeks are in the Queen's tent with Soredamors and the maidens.
Men and maids carry on a conversation:
> Meis Alixandres mot ne dist.
> Soredamors garde s'an prist,
> Qui pres de lui se fu assise.
> A sa meissele a sa main mise
> Et sanble que mout soit pansis.
>   (vv. 1375–1379.)

See also vv. 2998–2999 and 4339–4342.

> Thenceforth the fether in her lofty crest,
> Ruffed of love, gan lowly to availe,
> And her prowd portaunce and her princely gest,
> With which she earst tryumphed, now did quaile:
> Sad, solemne, sowre, and full of fancies fraile
> She woxe; yet wist she nether how, nor why;
> She wist not, silly mayd, what she did aile,
> Yet wist she was not well at ease perdy,
> Yet thought it was not love, but some melancholy.
>
> (*F. Q.*, III, ii, 27.)

Her nurse notes that she encloses herself in "dull corners" (*F. Q.*, III, ii, 31). Later, when she heard the Redcross Knight describe Artegall, Britomart

> Grew pensive through that amarous discourse,
> By which the Redcrosse Knight did earst display
> Her lovers shape and chevalrous aray.
>
> (*F. Q.*, III, iv, 5.)

Sir Termin loves a disdainful lady,

> From whom retourning sad and comfortlesse,

he and his companion fall in with Despair (*F. Q.*, I, ix, 28). The "pensife Scudamore" rides in search of his lost lady,

> Full of melancholie and sad misfare.
>
> (*F. Q.*, IV, vi, 2.)

Two knights despatched by Turpine to attack Prince Arthur espy him not far away,

> Ryding a softly pace with portance sad,
> Devizing of his love more then of daunger drad.
>
> (*F. Q.*, VI, vii, 6.)[16]

Even Neptune is made to assume the conventional air of dejection:

> The god himselfe did pensive seeme and sad,
> And hong adowne his head, as he did dreame.
>
> (*F. Q.*, III, xi, 41.)

---

[16] Cf. Petrarch:
> Solo e pensoso i più deserti campi
> Vo mesurando a passi tardi e lenti.
>   (Sonetto XXXV: "Solo e pensoso.")

See also the M. E. *Court of Love*, vv. 337–340.

The lover's slumbers are disturbed by dreams.[17]   When Britomart yielded to sleep,

> Streight way with dreames, and with fantastick sight
> Of dreadfull things, the same was put to flight,
> That oft out of her bed she did astart,
> As one with vew of ghastly feends affright.
> (*F. Q.*, III, ii, 29.)

Sir Scudamour, in search of Britomart and Amoret, stops overnight in the Cave of Care.   After much effort he falls asleep:

> Yet, in his soundest sleepe, his dayly feare
> His ydle braine gan busily molest,
> And made him dreame those two disloyall were:
> The things that day most minds, at night
> doe most appeare (*F. Q.*, IV, v, 43).[18]

Sometimes, however, the lover's dream is a sort of beatific vision.   In his Letter to Raleigh, Spenser tells us that he conceives Prince Arthur, after he had been brought up and educated by Timon, "to have seen in a dream or vision the Faery Queen, with whose excellent beauty ravished, he awaking resolved to seeke her out."[19]   In the first book of the *Faerie Queene* Arthur describes this vision.   He ranged the forest one day till weary of his sports he lay down to rest:

> Whiles every sence the humour sweet embayd,
> And slombring soft my hart did steale away,
> Me seemed, by my side a royall mayd
> Her daintie limbes full softly down did lay:
> So fayre a creature yet saw never sunny day.
>
> Most goodly glee and lovely blandishment
> She to me made, and badd me love her deare;
> For dearely sure her love was to me bent,
> As, when just time expired, should appeare.
> (*F. Q.*, I, ix, 13–14.)[20]

---

[17] Cf. the experience of the hero in *Amadis de Gaule*, London, 1619, II, ch. 6, p. 32.
[18] Cf. Gower, *Confessio Amantis*, IV, vv. 2891–2893.
[19] *Works*, ed. by Dodge, p. 136.
[20] The delicacy and spiritual quality of this vision suggest comparison with Petrarch's sonnet describing Laura's return after death to comfort the suffering lover:
        Del cibo onde 'l signor mio sempre a bonda.
                    (Sonetto CCCXLII.)

Love produces a chronic state of anxiety. The lover is a prey to doubts and fears of every sort.[21] He stands in awe of his lady. To the Redcross Knight Una is "his deare dreed" (*F. Q.*, I, vi, 2). The squire addresses Belphoebe as "dearest dred" (*F. Q.*, IV, viii, 17). When Artegall had sheared away Britomart's "ventayle" and had beheld her face,

> His powreless arme, benumbd with secret feare,
> From his revengefull purpose shronke abacke.
> (*F. Q.*, IV, vi, 21.)

In *Amoretti* 25 the poet asks why his "lyke dying lyfe" endures,

> Twixt feare and hope depending doubtfully.

Scudamour envies the happiness of the lovers in the Temple of Venus,

> That, being free from feare and gealosye,
> Might frankely there their loves desire possesse.
> (*F. Q.*, IV, x, 28.)[22]

He makes his way to Amoret:

> Whom soone as I beheld, my hart gan throb,
> And wade in doubt, what best were to be donne.
> (*F. Q.*, IV, x, 53.)

Finally, "shaking off all doubt and shamefast feare," he steps forward and takes her by the hand.

This fear often springs from the reputed fickleness of woman.[23] Hence the lover dreads a rival:

> The feare whereof, O how doth it torment
> His troubled mynd with more then hellish paine!
> (*Hymne in Honour of Love*, vv. 252–253.)

When Britomart had waited in vain for Artegall's return,

---

[21] Amorosus semper est timorosus.
(*De Amore*, ed. by Trojel, p. 311.)
Qui amer viaut, doter l'estuet,
Ou se ce non, amer ne puet.
(*Cligés*, vv. 3901–3902.)
Cf. Chaucer, *Book of the Duchess*, vv. 1211–1213.

[22] The lover's fear is personified in the court of love allegories. In the present case the knight is met by Doubt at the entrance to the castle and after he has entered his way is obstructed by Danger. Doubt and Fear appear also in the Masque of Cupid.
(*F. Q.*, III, xii, 10 and 12.)

[23] Cf. Petrarch, Sonetto CLXXXIII: "Se 'l dolce sguardo."

> She gan to cast in her misdoubtfull mynde
> A thousand feares, that love-sicke fancies
>   faine to fynde (*F. Q.*, V, vi, 3).

Her fear takes many forms,

> But most she did her troubled mynd molest,
> And secretly afflict with jealous feare,
> Least some new love had him from her possest.
>   (*F. Q.*, V, vi, 4.)[24]

In an enumeration of the evils which afflict lovers Spenser stresses the idea of fear:

> The gnawing envie, the hart-fretting feare,
> The vaine surmizes, the distrustfull showes,
> The false reports that flying tales doe beare,
> The doubts, the daungers, the delayes, the woes . . .
>   (*Hymne in Honour of Love*, vv. 259–262.)

The God of Love inspires terror in the beholder. In the Masque of Cupid he brandishes his darts and claps his wings,

> That all his many it affraide did make.
>   (*F. Q.*, III, xii, 23.)

Womanhood objects to Scudamour's wooing of Amoret in the Temple of Venus till she sees the image of Cupid emblazoned on the lover's shield:

> At sight thereof she was with terror queld,
> And said no more (*F. Q.*, IV, x, 55).

The lover's fear and his jealousy are scarcely separable. So much is implied in Spenser's use of the term "jealous fear." Jealousy is recommended by mediaeval writers on courtly love as a sure means of increasing the lover's affection.[25] Spenser, however, holds quite the opposite view. He denounces the passion as destructive of all love:

---

[24] Thus to man also is attributed fickleness of nature.

[25] The idea is probably derived from Ovid. See *Ars amatoria*, II, 445–446, and cf. Andreas Capellanus, *De Amore*, ed. by Trojel, p. 311 and Froissart, *Le Paradys d'Amour*, vv. 661–667.

O hatefull hellish snake! what Furie furst
Brought thee from balefull house of Proserpine,
Where in her bosome she thee long had nurst,
And fostred up with bitter milke of tine,
Fowle Gealosy! that turnest love divine
To joylesse dread, and mak'st the loving hart
With hatefull thoughts to languish and to pine,
And feed it selfe with selfe-consuming smart?
Of all the passions in the mind thou vilest art.

(F. Q., III, xi, 1.)

In the *Hymne in Honour of Love* he again attacks it as an enemy of love:

Yet is there one more cursed then they all,
That cancker worme, that monster Gelosie,
Which eates the hart, and feedes upon the gall,
Turning all loves delight to miserie,
Through feare of losing his felicitie.
Ah, gods! that ever ye that monster placed
In gentle love, that all his joyes defaced.

(vv. 266–272.)

One of Spenser's most repulsive creations is Malbecco, an embodiment of marital jealousy (F. Q., III, ix, 3 ff.). Sir Guyon rescues from Furor a young squire who had been driven by jealousy to slay his lady and poison his friend (F. Q., II, iv, 3 ff.). Love of Amyas makes Paeana jealous of Æmylia and Placidas (F. Q., IV, ix, 9). The shepherd Coridon resents Sir Calidore's attentions to Pastorella,

and even for gealousie
Was readie oft his owne hart to devoure,
Impatient of any paramoure (F. Q., VI, ix, 39).

Yet some of Spenser's noblest lovers suffer the pangs of jealousy. The Redcross Knight "burnt with gealous fire" when he saw the counterfeit Una in the embrace of a supposed lover (F. Q., I, ii, 5). Sir Scudamour is stirred to action against Britomart and Amoret by the false accusations of Ate,

The which like thornes did pricke his gealous hart,
And through his soule like poysned arrow persed.

(F. Q., IV, v, 31.)

Even Britomart is thrown into a jealous fit by the news that Artegall is held captive in the castle of the Amazon Radigund (*F. Q.*, V, vi, 11 ff.).

Another courtly commonplace so generally employed in love literature that it becomes trite and colorless is that love causes pain and suffering. It is found in Ovid, in Latin elegy, and in the poetry of the Alexandrines.[26] Provencal and Old French courtly poets harp upon love's *dolors*.[27] The strain is familiar to students of Petrarch and the French sonnet cycles. Passing to Elizabethan England it becomes the burden of the love lyrics of Oxford, Raleigh, Watson, and others. Spenser is not immune. In the January eclogue of the *Shepheardes Calender* Colin prays:

> Ye gods of love, that pitie lovers payne,
> (If any gods the paine of lovers pitie,)
> Looke from above, where you in joyes remaine,
> And bowe your eares unto my dolefull dittie.
>   (vv. 13–16.)

Even the lover's sheep are infected.[28] Colin finally seeks surcease of "long affliction" and "ease of paine" in singing Rosalind's praises (*Colin Clout*, vv. 943–946). Thus the pastoral and the courtly conventions unite in stressing the lover's pain.[29]

In the *Teares of the Muses* Erato bids gentle lovers turn their eulogies into elegies:

> Such as ye wont, when as those bitter stounds,
> Of raging love first gan you to torment,
> And launch your hearts with lamentable wounds
> Of secret sorrow and sad languishment,
> Before your loves did take you unto grace;
> Those now renew, as fitter for this place.
>   (vv. 373–378.)

---

[26] See *Ars amatoria*, I, 736–738 and cf. Schrötter, *Ovid und die Troubadours*, p. 64.

[27] An example from William IX, Count of Poitou, is typical:
> e sapchatz, quar tan vos am,
> tem que la dolors me ponia,
> si no·m faitz dreg dels tortz qu'ie·us clam.
>   (Appel, *Prov. Chrest.*, p. 52.)

[28] See the eclogue for August, vv. 17–18. No better illustration of the imitative character of the early Elizabethan courtly poetry could be found than this striving for originality which results in palpable absurdity.

[29] Cf. *F. Q.*, VI, ix, 10 and *F. Q.*, VI, x, 1.

The lover in the *Hymne in Honour of Beautie* seeks grace for his withered heart "after long sorrow and consuming smart" (v. 8). In the *Hymne in Honour of Love* the poet says:

> Thou that hast never lov'd canst not beleeve
> Least part of th' evils which poore lovers greeve.
> (vv. 257–258.)

These evils he enumerates and concludes that they,

> With thousands more then any tongue can tell,
> Doe make a lovers life a wretches hell (vv. 264–265).

The conventional note of woe which runs through the *Amoretti* is sounded as early as the second sonnet:

> Unquiet thought, whom at the first I bred
> Of th' inward bale of my love pined hart,
> And sithens have with sighes and sorrowes fed,
> Till greater then my wombe thou woxen art:
> Breake forth at length out of the inner part,
> In which thou lurkest lyke to vipers brood,
> And seeke some succour, both to ease my smart
> And also to sustayne thy selfe with food.

The Redcross Knight suffers grief and anguish over the supposed unfaithfulness of Una (*F. Q.*, I, ii, 6 and 12). Sir Scudamour suffers "long sorrow" over the loss of Amoret until succored by Britomart.

The pain of absence is especially severe.[30] In *Amoretti* 52 the poet says that he always leaves his lady as a prisoner who has lost the field:

> So doe I now my selfe a prisoner yeeld
> To sorrow and to solitary paine:
> From presence of my dearest deare exylde,
> Long while alone in languor to remaine.

---

[30] Amadis of Gaul, separated from Oriana, "endured an exceeding torment which the more he thought to hide the more it appeared." (*Amadis de Gaule*, London, 1619, II, ch. 2, p. 6.) In the M. E. *Court of Love* the lover is commanded, in the lady's absence,

> To wring and wail, to turn, and sigh and grone (v. 493).

The sequence closes with the feeling of separation, absence, and loss dominant.[31]   In *Daphnaida* the lover appeals to the sympathy of those who are exiled from the presence of their ladies as well as those who bask in the sunlight of favor (vv. 505–515).

However cold and reserved the lady may appear, she, too, suffers the pangs of love.[32]   When the Redcross Knight had deserted Una, the latter was

> sore grieved in her gentle brest,
> He so ungently left her, whome she loved best.
> (*F. Q.*, I, ii, 8.)

When she learned of his sufferings her heart was almost rent in twain by "sorrowfull assay" (*F. Q.*, I, vii, 27).   Britomart,

> by long triall of the inward griefe,
> Wherewith imperious love her hart did vexe,
> Could judge what paines doe loving harts perplexe.
> (*F. Q.*, III, i, 54.)

Amoret and Florimell suffered "unworthie paine" on account of love (*F. Q.*, IV, i, 1).   Both Radigund and her maid Clarinda were tormented with anguish for love of Artegall (*F. Q.*, V, v, 27–28, 44).   To such an extent is this true that the poet in one place asks the God of Love what glory he finds

> In feeble ladies tyranning so sore.
> (*F. Q.*, IV, vii, 1.)

In mediaeval courtly poetry suffering is commonly regarded as a condition or, at least, as a necessary accompaniment of love.[33]

---

[31] See especially the last three sonnets.

[32] Cf. the effect of love on Soredamors in Chrétien's *Cligés*, vv. 878–884.

[33] The idea is found in Old Italian literature:
> Neiente vale amar senza penare
> Chi vuol amar conviene mal patire.
> (*Poeti del prim. sec.* I, p. 194.)

In the *Romaunt of the Rose* the God of Love says to the lover:
> And first of o thing warne I thee
> That peyne and gret adversite
> He mote endure and eke travaile
> That shal me serve without faile (vv. 2009–2012).

Cf. Bédier, *De Nicolao Museto*, p. 29.

Spenser states the point with epigrammatic force:

> For lovers heaven must passe by sorrowes hell.
> (F. Q., IV, vi, 32.)

The lover, therefore, not only submits to grievous torment but actually welcomes it. Pain itself becomes sweet. Thus arises the paradoxical *süssen Schmerz*.[34] Spenser employs the device in *Amoretti* 42:

> The love which me so cruelly tormenteth
> So pleasing is in my extreamest paine,
> That all the more my sorrow it augmenteth,
> The more I love and doe embrace my bane.

Britomart saw in the magic mirror the image of Artegall:

> Whereof did grow her first engraffed payne,
> Whose root and stalke so bitter yet did taste,
> That, but the fruit more sweetness did contayne,
> Her wretched dayes in dolour she mote waste,
> And yield the pray of love to lothsome death
> at last (*F. Q.*, III, ii, 17).

Not all of Spenser's lovers, however, are so sanguine as to the pre-eminence of the sweet over the bitter in love. In the January eclogue of the *Shepheardes Calender* Colin dolefully complains:

> Ah, God! that love should breede both joy and payne!
> (v. 54.)

More decided is Thomalin's emblem at the close of the March eclogue:

> Of hony and of gaule in love there is store:
> The honye is much, but the gaule is more.

---

[34] See Schrötter, *Ovid und die Troubadours*, pp. 71 ff. and Chrétien's *Cligès*, vv. 3070–3073. This method of defining love by the use of contradictory epithets, though it became a literary fad, never reached the absurd lengths in Spenser that it attained in earlier courtly poets. Cf. Alanus de Insulis, *De Planctu Naturae*, tr. Moffat, pp. 46 ff.; Novati, F., *Attraverso il Medio Evo*, 1905, p. 69 (note); *Romaunt of the Rose*, vv. 2301–2303.

Sir Scudamour holds a similar opinion:

> True he it said, what ever man it sayd,
> That love with gall and hony doth abound,
> But if the one be with the other wayd,
> For every dram of hony therein found,
> A pound of gall doth over it redound.
> . . . .
> For though sweet love to conquer glorious bee,
> Yet is the paine thereof much greater then the fee.
> <div align="right">(<i>F. Q.</i>, IV, x, 1, 3.)</div>

Elsewhere the poet gives a reason for this:

> The joyes of love, if they should ever last,
> Without affliction or disquietnesse,
> That worldly chaunces doe amongst them cast,
> Would be on earth too great a blessednesse,
> Liker to heaven then mortall wretchednesse.
> Therefore the winged god, to let men weet
> That here on earth is no sure happinesse,
> A thousand sowres hath tempred with one sweet,
> To make it seeme more deare and dainty,
> <div align="right">as is meet (<i>F. Q.</i>, VI, xi, 1).</div>

The lover's sufferings cause him to complain continually of his lady's cruelty and to plead for mercy. In the *Romance of the Rose* the lover is urged by the God of Love to try to soften his lady's heart by making songs and complaints.[35] In the June eclogue of the *Shepheardes Calender* Spenser says that if he had Chaucer's skill he would teach the trees and woods to wail his woes:

> Then should my plaints, causd of discurtesee,
> As messengers of all my painfull plight,
> Flye to my love where ever that she bee,
> And pierce her heart with poynt of worthy wight,
> As shee deserves, that wrought so deadly spight.
> (vv. 97–101.)

In the concluding plea of *Colin Clouts Come Home Again* he begs Rosalind to grant

---

[35] Among eke for thy lady sake
Songes and complayntes that thou make
For that wole meuen in hir herte
Whanne they reden of thy smerte (vv. 2325–2328).

> To simple swaine, sith her I may not love,
> Yet that I may her honour paravant
> And praise her worth, though far my wit above.
>   (vv. 940–942.)

In *An Hymne in Honour of Love* the poet says that love's flame consumes wretched lovers:

> Thenceforth they playne, and make ful piteous mone
> Unto the author of their balefull bane (vv. 127–128).

So in *An Hymne in Honour of Beautie* the poet appeals to his lady:

> And you, faire Venus dearling, my deare dread,
> Fresh flowre of grace, great goddesse of my life,
> When your fair eyes these fearefull lines shal read,
> Deigne to let fall one drop of dew reliefe,
> That may recure my harts long pyning griefe,
> And shew what wondrous powre your beauty hath,
> That can restore a damned wight from death.
>   (vv. 281–287.)[36]

In *Amoretti* 10 the poet complains to the God of Love of the "proud hart" and "high look" of his "tyrannesse." Hence he proposes to lay "incessant battery" to her heart by means of

> Playnts, prayers, vowes, ruth, sorrow, and dismay.
>   (*Amoretti* 14.)

Again he pleads:

> Tell me, when shall these wearie woes have end,
> Or shall their ruthlesse torment never cease,
> But al my dayes in pining languor spend,
> Without hope of aswagement or release?
>   (*Amoretti* 36.)

In *Amoretti* 49 he asks:

[36] Cf. Guido delle Colonne:
> Se di me non le prende pietanza
> Ben morrò certamenta.
> Per neente mi cangiò lo suo talento,
> Ond 'io tormento, e vivo in gran dotanza,
> E son di molte pene sofferente.
>   (*Poeti del primo seculo,* vol. I, pp. 183–184.)

> Fayre cruell, why are ye so fierce and cruell?

Continuing he begs her to use her power against her enemies,

> But him that at your footstoole humbled lies,
> With merciful regard, give mercy too.[37]

In *Amoretti* 55 he compares her beauty and her cruelty and marvels that she could be so "cruell faire." He concludes by praying her to

> Be lyke in mercy as in all the rest.

But apparently his pleas are unavailing, for in *Amoretti* 57 he breaks out again:

> Ye cruell one! what glory can be got,
> In slaying him that would live gladly yours?
> Make peace therefore, and graunt me timely grace,
> That al my wounds wil heale in little space.[38]

The lovers in the *Faerie Queene* also complain of their hard lot and pray for relief. Paridell protested his love for Hellenore,

> Saying, but if she mercie would him give,
> That he mote algates dye, yet did his death forgive.
> (*F. Q.*, III, x, 7.)

Prince Arthur, in pursuit of Florimell, often wished that

> that lady faire mote bee
> His Faery Queene, for whom he did complain.
> (*F. Q.*, III, iv, 54.)

---

[37] Cf. Froissart (*Le Paradys d'Amour*, vv. 1483–1487):
The lover meets his lady in the meadow and kneels before her:
> Dame, di je, Amours me commande
> Que nostre grasce je demande,
> Car j'ai jà un lonc temps langi
> Sans avoir grasce ne merci,
> Joie, esperance ne confort.

[38] Cf. *Chaucer's Dream*:
> Fairest of faire, and goodliest on live,
> All my secret to you I plaine, and shrive,
> Requiring grace and of complaint,
> To be healed or martyred as a saint,
> For by my trouth I sweare, and by this booke,
> Ye may both heale, and slea me with a looke.

(Chalmers, *English Poets*, London, 1810, vol. I, p. 394.)
See also Petrarch, CCXXXIX: "Là vèr' l'aurora," vv. 6–12, and *Trionfo d'Amore*, Canto II, vv. 145–150.

Venus, in search of her lost son, came to court and found there many who complained of Cupid's cruel treatment; and in city and country the same cry was raised (*F. Q.,* III, vi, 13–15). The lovers in the Temple of Venus chanted the same refrain:

> And all about her altar, scattered lay
> Great sorts of lovers piteously complayning,
> Some of their losse, some of their loves delay,
> Some of their pride, some paragons disdayning,
> Some fearing fraud, some fraudulently fayning,
> As every one had cause of good or ill.
> (*F. Q.,* IV, x, 43.)

Mirabella confessed to cruel treatment of many who grieved for love of her,

> Complayning out on me, that would not on them rew.
> (*F. Q.,* VI, viii, 20.)

Thus she triumphed long in lovers' pain,

> And sitting carelesse on the scorners stoole,
> Did laugh at those that did lament and plaine.
> (*F. Q.,* VI, viii, 21.)

Against such cruelty the poet warns all ladies:

> But cruelty and hardnesse from you chace,
> That all your other praises will deface,
> And from you turne the love of men to hate.
> (*F. Q.,* VI, viii, 2.)[39]

In spite of plaints and prayers, however, the lady always yielded her favor slowly and with seeming reluctance, evidently mindful of the dictum stated in the *Romance of the Rose* that

> A man loveth more tendirly
> The thyng that he hath bought most dere.[40]
> (vv. 2738–2739.)

Thus the lady's obduracy cultivated in the lover the indispensable virtues of patience and perseverance.

---

[39] Note that Cruelty is a character in the Masque of Cupid (*F. Q.,* III, xii, 19).

[40] The principle had been stated earlier by Andreas Capellanus:
Facilis perceptio contemptibilem reddit amorem, difficilis eum carum facet haberi (*De Amore,* ed. by Trojel, p. 310). Cf. Ovid, *Ars amatoria,* III, 579.

Prince Arthur told how he saw the vision of the Faerie Queene and added:

> From that day forth I cast in carefull mynd,
> To seeke her out with labor and long tyne,
> And never vow to rest, till her I fynd:
> Nyne monethes I seek in vain, yet ni'll that
>   vow unbynd (*F. Q.,* I, ix, 12).

Artegall wooed Britomart,

> And with meeke service and much suit did lay
> Continuall siege unto her gentle hart.[41]
>   (*F. Q.,* IV, vi, 40.)

Sir Calidore was persistent in his wooing of Pastorella:

> Ne any paines ne perill did he shonne,
> By which he might her to his love allure,
> And liking in her yet untamed heart procure.
>   (*F. Q.,* VI, x, 32.)

As the poet himself, speaking through Sir Scudamour, puts it:

> Unworthy they of grace, whom one deniall
> Excludes from fairest hope, withouten further triall.
>   (*F. Q.,* IV, x, 17.)

Thus, says the poet in *An Hymne in Honour of Love,* the God of Love tests his subjects that, having found love difficult to win, they may cherish it the more:

> For things hard gotten men more dearely deeme.
>   (v. 168.)

Love results in captivity. The lover becomes a prisoner in the hands of his lady or of Love himself. The figure is a

---

[41] Cf. *Court of Love:*
> The *eighth* statut, to my rememberaunce,
> Was, To speke, and pray my lady dere,
> With hourly labour and gret attendaunce,
> Me for to love with all her herte entere.
>   (vv. 351–354.)

commonplace in the courtly system.[42] In the December eclogue
of the *Shepheardes Calender* Colin complains that in the spring
of his life the shepherd's god bereft him of his freedom:

> My freedome lorne, my life he lefte to mone (v. 52).

In *Amoretti* 29 the poet says of his lady that by the token of
victory which he gave her she

> Accoumpts my self her captive quite forlorne.[43]

As a prisoner the lover is bound with chains or fetters.
Says the troubadour nobleman William IX:

> e ia per plag que m'en mueva,
> no·m solvera de son liam.[44]

In *Amoretti* 12 the lover complains that in a time of truce with
his lady's eyes he was surprised by an ambush:

> Who me captiving streight with rigorous wrong,
> Have ever since me kept in cruell bands.

Often it is the lover's heart that is held in bondage.[45]
In *Amoretti* 42 the lover yields to his mistress his "poore
captyved hart":

> The which, that it from her may never start,
> Let her, yf please her, bynd with adamant chayne,
> And from all wandring loves, which mote pervart
> His safe assurance, strongly it restrayne.

---

[42] See, for example, Bernart de Ventadorn in Appel, *Prov. Chrest.*, pp. 57 and 58;
Schmidt, E., Reinmar von Hagenau, in *Quellen und Forschungen*, vol. IV, p. 87; Chrétien
de Troyes, *Yvain*, vv. 1941–1942; Guillaume de Machaut, *Dit du Vergier, in Œuvres*, ed.
by P. Tarbé, Reims and Paris, 1849, p. 19; and the *Romance of the Rose*, vv. 2766–2768,
where the God of Love says to the lover:
> And so for lovers in her wenyng
> Whiche love hath shitte in his prisoun
> Good hope is her salvacioun.
    Cf. Schrötter, *Ovid und die Troubadours*, pp. 53 ff.

[43] Cf. Petrarch, Canzone XXII: "Nel dolce tempo," vv. 7–9, and Sonetto CI: "Lasso,
ben so che dolorose prede."

[44] Appel, *Prov. Chrest.*, p. 52. Cf. Andreas Capellanus:
> Dicitur autem amor ab ama verbo, quod significat capere vel capi. Nam qui
> amat, captus est cupidinis vinculis aliumque desiderat suo capere hamo.
> (*De Amore*, ed. by Trojel, p. 9.)

[45] Canzonetta geoiosa,
> Va all fior di Soria,
> A quella che in prigione ha lo
>   mio core (*Poeti del prim. sec.*, I, p. 122).

In *Amoretti* 10 he says that his lady massacres with her eyes and "humbled harts brings captive" to the God of Love. In the *Hymne in Honour of Love* it is this god who has made his heart a prisoner:

> Love, that long since hast to thy mighty powre
> Perforce subdude my poore captived hart.
> (vv. 1–2.)

In the *Hymne in Honour of Beautie* the poet prays Venus

> That she, whose conquering beautie doth captive
> My trembling hart in her eternall chaine,
> One drop of grace at length will to me give.
> (vv. 275–277.)

Sometimes the lover is snared, as the fly is caught in the spider's web.[46] In *Amoretti* 37 the poet fears lest the net with which his lady binds her hair may be a golden snare to entangle his eyes and thus capture his heart:

> Take heed therefore, myne eyes, how ye doe stare
> Henceforth too rashly on that guilefull net,
> In which if ever ye entrapped are,
> Out of her bands ye by no meanes shall get.
> Fondnesse it were for any, being free,
> To covet fetters, though they golden be.[47]

In consequence of his sufferings and hard usage as his lady's prisoner, the lover is reduced to despair.[48] Colin's emblem for the June eclogue of the *Shepheardes Calender* is—

> Già speme spenta.[49]

---

[46] See Long, P. W., "Spenser's Muiopotmos," *Mod. Lang. Rev.,* 1914, pp. 457 ff. Dr. Long argues that the poem is, in allegorical form, a courtly compliment to Lady Carey, to whom it is dedicated—the poet himself being the innocent butterfly and her ladyship the crafty spider.

[47] Cf. *F. Q.,* II, xii, 77. The conceit is a refinement upon a mediaeval convention— Elizabethan rather than purely court of love. See Lee, S., *Elizabethan Sonnets,* vol. I, p. xciv.

[48] In the *Romance of the Rose* the lover is wounded by an arrow shot by the God of Love. Thereupon, he says,
> So nygh I drowe to desperaunce
> I rought of deth ne of lyf (vv. 1872–1873).
Cf. Petrarch, Sonetto CXXIV: "Amor, fortuna."

[49] In the gloss to the emblem E. K. says: You remember that in the fyrst Æglogue, Colin's poesie was *Anchora speme*: for that as then there was hope of favour to be found in tyme. But nowe being cleane forlorne and rejected of her, as whose hope, that was, is cleane extinguished and turned into despeyre, he renounceth all comfort, and hope of good-nesse to come: which is all the meaning of thys embleme.

In *Colin Clouts Come Home Again* the poet says that he did
not sing of love when he and Raleigh sang together,

> For love had me forlorne, forlorne of me,
> That made me in that desart chose to dwell.
> (vv. 90–91.)

Belphoebe saves the life of Timias, who immediately falls in
love with his fair rescuer:

> What bootes it him from death to be unbownd,
> To be captived in endlesse duraunce
> Of sorrow and despeyre without aleggeaunce?
> (F. Q., III, v, 42.)[50]

Scudamour is found by Britomart in despair over the loss of
Amoret (F. Q., III, xi, 9 ff.). Sir Trevisan and Sir Terwin,
two knightly lovers languishing in disfavor, are accosted on the
road by Despair himself.[51] When the "cursed wight" learned
of their misfortunes in love,

> With wounding words, and termes of foule repriefe,
> He pluckt from us all hope of dew reliefe,
> That earst us held in love of lingring life:
> Then hopelesse hartlesse, gan the cunning thiefe
> Perswade us dye, to stint all further strife:
> To me he lent this rope, to him a rusty knife.
> (F. Q., I, ix, 29.)

From the mental and temperamental effects of love we
pass now to the resultant physical or "pathological" symptoms.
Here, again, we find that Spenser has been definitely influenced
by courtly ideals.

In the first place, the lover stricken with a passion for his
lady experiences a burning sensation within. It is the flame

---

[50] Cf. the lover in Caulier's *L'Hospital d'Amours*, who, having been rejected by his
lady, goes home in despair:
> En ce seul vouloir de mourir
> Passoye toute la nuitie,
> Riens ne me povoit secourir.
> (*Œuvres de Chartier*, ed. by Du Chesne, p. 723.)

[51] A familiar figure in mediaeval literature, Despair is inevitably introduced into the
court of love allegories. In Lydgate's *Temple of Glas* the knight speaks of the struggle in
his breast between the abstractions Hope and Despair. In the M. E. *Court of Love* Despair
is an attendant at court. See Carpenter, F. I., "Spenser's Cave of Despair," *Mod. Lang.
Notes*, vol. 12, pp. 257 ff.

of desire, the fire of love that scorches and sears his very vitals.[52] In the December eclogue of the *Shepheardes Calender* Colin says that the springtime of his love passed,

> And sommer season sped him to display
> (For Love then in the Lyons house did dwell)
> The raging fyre that kindled at his ray.
>
> (vv. 56–58.)

In the gloss E. K. remarks that the meaning of the allegory is "that love in him wrought an extraordinarie heate of lust." In the *Hymne in Honour of Love* the poet says that "now t' asswage the force of this new flame" he will sing praises to the God of Love (v. 8). In the *Hymne in Honour of Beautie* he says to the god:

> Whylest seeking to aslake thy raging fyre,
> Thou in me kindlest much more great desyre.
>
> (vv. 4–5.)

The poet begs Venus to beautify his hymn:

> That both to thee, to whom I meane it most,
> And eke to her, whose faire immortall beame
> Hath darted fyre into my feeble ghost,
> That now it wasted is with woes extreame,
> It may so please that she at length will streame
> Some deaw of grace into my withered hart,
> After long sorrow and consuming smart.
>
> (vv. 22–28.)

Later, in the *Hymne of Heavenly Love* Spenser says to those who had misinterpreted the first two hymns:

> And ye that wont with greedy vaine desire
> To read my fault, and wondring at my flame,
> To warme your selves at my wide sparckling fire,

---

[52] Uror, et in vacuo pectore regnat Amor.
(Ovid, *Amores*, I, 1.)
Pus tot jorn m'en falh aizina,
No m meravilh s'ieu m' aflam.
(Jaufre Rudel, in Raynouard, *Poésies des Troubadours*, Paris, 1818, vol. 3, p. 99.)
The more thine herte brenneth in fier
The more thine herte is in desire
For who considreth everydeel
It may be likned wondir well
The peyne of love unto a fere.
(*Romance of the Rose*, vv. 2467–2471.)
Cf. also M. E. *Court of Love*, vv. 883–885, and Petrarch, LV: "Quel foco."

> Sith now that heat is quenched, quench my blame,
> And in her ashes shrowd my dying shame.
>
> (vv. 15–19.)

The convention recurs in the *Faerie Queene*. Britomart, in love with Artegall, says to her nurse:

> For no no usuall fire, no usuall rage
> Yt is, O nourse, which on my life doth feed,
> And sucks the blood which from my hart doth bleed.
>
> (*F. Q.*, III, ii, 37.)

Hellenore shows to Paridell a "desire her inward flame to slake" (*F. Q.*, III, ix, 31). Malecasta, the lady of Castle Joyous, becomes enamoured of Britomart:

> Her fickle hart conceived hasty fyre,
> Like sparkes of fire which fall in sclender flex,
> That shortly brent into extreme desyre,
> And ransackt all her veines with passion entyre.
>
> (*F. Q.*, III, i, 47.)

To her love was

> But as a cole to kindle fleshly flame,

which she was so ill able to conceal that she soon revealed her desire by lamentations and complaints,

> The outward sparkes of her inburning fire.
>
> (*F. Q.*, III, i, 50 and 53.)

Fradubio, metamorphosed into a tree by enchantment, was yet able to tell his story to the Redcross Knight:

> In prime of youthly yeares, when corage hott
> The fire of love and joy of chevalree
> First kindled in my brest, it was my lott
> To love this gentle lady—(*F. Q.*, I, ii, 35).

Claribell was

> enraged rife
> With fervent flames, and loved out of measure.
>
> (*F. Q.*, IV, ix, 21.)

Many a shepherd honored Pastorella and "burnt in her love"
(*F. Q.*, VI, ix, 10). Sir Calidore, also, falling in love with the
shepherdess, accompanied her to the fields:

> So for to quench his fire, he did it more augment.
> (*F. Q.*, VI, ix, 34.)

Mirabella's beauty likewise

> did kindle lovely fire
> In th' harts of many a knight, and many
> a gentle squire (*F. Q.*, VI, vii, 28).[53]

The inflammatory function of love is allegorized in the picture
of Desire, a character in the Masque of Cupid:

> Twixt both his hands few sparks he close did strayne,
> Which still he blew, and kindled busily,
> That soone they life conceiv'd and forth in flames
> did fly (*F. Q.*, III, xii, 9).

That the threadbare metaphor was rapidly losing force
through vain repetition is, however, evident from attempts
made even before Spenser to elaborate it by exaggeration. In
the *Venus la Deesse d'Amor* the lover cries to the nightingale:

> Rousegnols sire, ie sui cil qui languist,
> Li feus d'amor mon cuer arst et bruist (29).[54]

In *Amoretti* 32 Spenser says:

> Yet cannot all these flames in which I fry
> Her hart, more harde then yron, soft a whit.

In the *Faerie Queene* the maid Clarinda, herself enamoured
of Artegall, turned the trust placed in her by Radigund

> To feeding of her private fire, which boyld
> Her inward brest, and in her entrayles fryde.
> (*F. Q.*, V, v, 53.)

---

[53] Cf. the "raging fire of love to woman kind."
(*F. Q.*, IV, ix, 1.)

[54] Cf. Guillaume de Machaut's *Dit du Vergier*, where the God of Love says that when
Desire attacks the lover,
    Il l'art, il l'alume; il l'esprent . . . .
                    (*Œuvres*, ed. by Tarbé p. 27.)

To "burn," "inflame," and "scorch" Spenser adds "boil" and "fry." The logical outcome of this tendency is Donne and the metaphysical school.

Further, love not only inflames but it also chills. Hence the lover experiences fluctuations of heat and cold.[55] In the January eclogue of the *Shepheardes Calender* Colin complains:

> Such rage as winters reigneth in my heart,
> My life bloud friesing with unkindly cold.
> (vv. 25–26.)[56]

In *Amoretti* 30 Spenser makes a different application of the figure:

> My love is lyke to yse, and I to fyre;
> How comes it then that this her cold so great
> Is not dissolv'd through my so hot desyre,
> But harder growes the more I her entreat?
> Or how comes it that my exceeding heat
> Is not delayd by her hart frosen cold,
> But that I burne much more in boyling sweat,
> And feele my flames augmented manifold?
> What more miraculous thing may be told,
> That fire, which all things melts, should harden yse,
> And yse, which is congeald with sencelesse cold,
> Should kindle fyre by wonderful devyse?
> Such is the powre of love in gentle mind,
> That it can alter all the course of kynd.

The poet does not here contrast the extremes of heat and cold produced in himself by love but compares the fire of his own passion with the iciness of his lady's reserve. This adaptation of the convention is Petrarchan.[57]

---

[55] In the *Romance of the Rose* the God of Love says to the lover:
Thou shalte no whyle be in o state
But whylom colde and whilom hate (vv. 2397–2398).
    Cf. Petrarch, Sonetto CXXXIV: "Pace non trovo." See also Raleigh's introduction to his edition of Hoby's translation of Castiglione's *Il Cortegiano* (London 1900, p. 75).

[56] The suggestion that the cold is unnatural and abnormal is regularly a part of the convention. In the *Romance of the Rose* the God of Love sent an arrow to the heart of the lover:
And therwith all such colde me hente
That under clothes warme and softe
Sithen that day I have chevered ofte (vv. 1730–1732).
In Gower's *Confessio Amantis* (VI, 249) the lover says:
In cold I brenne and frese in hete.
    Elizabethan examples of this paradox are abundant. See especially Wyatt, in *Tottel's Miscellany* (Arber Reprint), pp. 39, 40, and 45.

[57] Ite, caldi sospiri al freddo core;
Rompete il ghiaccio che pietà contende.
(Sonetto CLIII: "Ite, caldi sospiri.")
    See also Lee, *Elizabethan Sonnets*, vol. I, p. xciv and Borland, L., *The Influence of Marot on English Poetry of the 16th Century*, U. of C. Diss., Chicago, 1913, p. 75.

The vicissitudes of the lover's fortunes keep him in a state of nervous restlessness—or *malaise*—accompanied with loss of sleep. Thus in the *Romance of the Rose* the lover complains:

> A man to lyen hath gret disese
> Which may not slepe ne reste in ese.[58]
> (vv. 2631–2632.)

In the August eclogue of the *Shepheardes Calender* the lovelorn Colin says:

> I hate the house, since thence my love did part,
> Whose waylefull want debarres myne eyes from sleepe.
> (vv. 161–162.)

He decides to remain in the forest till the end:

> So shall I not augment,
> With sight of such a chaunge, my restlesse woe.
> (vv. 171–172.)

In *Amoretti* 86 the poet says:

> Since I did leave the presence of my love,
> Many long weary dayes I have outworne,
> And many nights, that slowly seemd to move
> Thyr sad protract from evening untill morne.
> For when as day the heaven doth adorne,
> I wish that night the noyous day would end:
> And when as night hath us of light forlorne,
> I wish that day would shortly reascend.

Cupid suffers neither gods nor men to rest:

> But when thou art disposed cruelly,
> Theyr sleepe thou doost molest (*Epigram* IV).

Sir Scudamour in the House of Care lay a long while expecting,

---

[58] Attenuent juvenum vigilatae corpora noctes.
        (*Ovid, Ars am.,* I, 735.)
   See also *Amores,* I, ii, 1–4.
        Ben sai la nueg quan mi despuelh
        El lieg que no i dormirai re;
        Lo dormir pert, quar ieu lo m tuelh,
        Domna, quan de vos mi sove.
(Bernard de Ventadorn, in Raynouard, *Poesies des Troubadours,* Paris, 1818, vol. 3, p. 66.)

> When gentle sleepe his heavie eyes would close.

But no matter how often he changed his position,

> He by no meanes could wished ease obtaine.
>> (F. Q., IV, v, 40.)

After meeting Colin Clout, Sir Calidore returned to Pastorella, whose love "had bred his restlesse paine" (F. Q., VI, x, 31). Thus the lover's anxieties and fears make him imagine

> Sights never seene, and thousand shadowes vaine,
> To breake his sleepe and waste his ydle braine.
>> (Hymne in Honour of Love, vv. 255–256.)

The lady also suffers the same effects.[59]   Una weeps all night for loss of the Redcross Knight:

> All night she thinks too long, and often
> lookes for light (F. Q., I, iii, 15).

After beholding Artegall's figure in Merlin's magic mirror Britomart lay down to sleep,

> But sleepe full far away from her did fly.
>> (F. Q., III, ii, 28.)

Later, en route to rescue Artegall from Radigund, she spent the night in the house of Dolon:

> There all that night remained Britomart,
> Restlesse, recomfortlesse, with heart deepe grieved,
> Not suffering the least twinckling sleepe to start
> Into her eye, which th' heart mote have relieved,
> But if the least appear'd, her eyes she streight
> reprieved (F. Q., V, vi, 24).

Becoming infatuated with Britomart,

> Faire Malecasta, whose engrieved spright
> Could find no rest in such perplexed plight,
> Lightly arose out of her wearie bed.
>> (F. Q., III, i, 59.)

---

[59] In Chrétien's *Cligés* Soredamors is secretly in love with Alexander:
> Tote nuit est an si grant painne,
> Qu 'ele ne dort ne repose (vv. 876–877).
Cf. *Yvain*, vv. 2756–2759.

The lover's sleeplessness is frequently attended with loss of appetite.[60] Both symptoms are recognized conventions of Elizabethan courtly poetry.[61] In Book IV of the *Faerie Queene* Marinell, having fallen in love with Florimell,

> Ne dayly food did take, ne nightly sleepe.
> (*F. Q.*, IV, xii, 19.)

Sighs and tears are among the most common of the conventional effects of love. In the *Romance of the Rose* the God of Love warns the lover that he shall dream in vain of possessing his lady:

> Thanne shalt thou sighe and wepe faste (v. 2580).

In Chrétien's *Cligés* Fenice grieves for her lover who is absent in Britain:

> Sovant plore, sovant sospire (v. 4359).[62]

In the January eclogue of the *Shepheardes Calender* Colin thus complains:

> The blossome which my braunch of youth did beare
> With breathed sighes is blowne away and blasted;
> And from mine eyes the drizling teares descend,
> As on your boughes the ysicles depend (vv. 39–42).

In the August eclogue the lover says:

> Thou pleasaunt spring hast luld me oft a sleepe,
> Whose streames my trickling teares did ofte augment.
> (vv. 155–156.)

---

[60] Andreas Capellanus says:
    Minus dormit et edit, quem amoris cogitatio vexat.
        (*De Amore*, ed. by Trojel, p. 311.)
Cf. *De Venus la Deesse d'Amor*, 161.
[61] Long, *Elizabethan Courtly Love*, ch. II.
[62] See also vv. 885–890; and cf. Ovid, *Ars amatoria*, I, 659–660 and III, 675; Cercamon, in Appel, *Prov. Chrest.*, p. 53, vv. 4–5; *De Phillide et Flora*, vv. 33–34; *De Venus la Deesse d'Amor*, 55; Guillaume de Machaut, *Dit du Vergier*, *Œuvres*, ed. by Tarbé, p. 24; Petrarch, Sonetto XVII: "Piovommi amare"; and Wyatt, *Tottel's Miscellany* (Arber), p. 45.

In *Amoretti* 18 the poet says:

> But when I pleade, she bids me play my part,
> And when I weep, she says teares are but water,
> And when I sigh, she sayes I know the art,
> And when I waile, she turnes hir selfe to laughter.

The Lady Una, wandering in search of the Redcross Knight, seeks rest overnight in the cottage of Blind Devotion:

> In stead of rest, she does lament, and weepe
> For the late losse of her deare loved knight,
> And sighes, and grones, and evermore does steepe
> Her tender brest in bitter teares all night.
> <div align="right">(<i>F. Q.</i>, I, iii, 15.)</div>

When Prince Arthur awoke from his vision of the Faerie Queene and "found her place devoyd," he was in great sorrow,

> And washed all her place with watry eyen.
> <div align="right">(<i>F. Q.</i>, I, ix, 15.)</div>

Sansloy captured Una and sought to court her by "looking lovely and oft sighing sore" (*F. Q.*, I, vi, 4). Paridell, in paying court to Hellenore, followed a similar method:

> He sigh'd, he sobd, he swownd, he perdy dyde. . . .
> He wept, and wayld, and false laments belyde.
> <div align="right">(<i>F. Q.</i>, III, x, 7.)</div>

The lady of Castle Joyous, unable to conceal her love for Britomart, broke all bounds,

> And all attonce discovered her desire
> With sighes, and sobs, and plaints, and
>   piteous griefe (*F. Q.*, III, i, 53).

She entered Britomart's chamber at night,

> Ne any noise she made, ne word she spake,
> But inly sigh'd (*F. Q.*, III, i, 61).

After Britomart had seen Artegall's image in Merlin's magic mirror sleep fled from her:

> In stead thereof sad sighes and sorrowes deepe
> Kept watch and ward about her warily,
> That nought she did but wayle, and often steepe
> Her dainty couch with teares, which closely
>   she did weepe (*F. Q.*, III, ii, 28).

Having set forth to find him, she fell in with the Redcross Knight, who asked her why she had come so far from her own land:

> Thereat she sighing softly, had no powre
> To speake a while (*F. Q.*, III, ii, 5).

She came to the sea and called upon Neptune for aid:

> Then sighing softly sore, and inly deepe,
> She shut up all her plaint in privy griefe.
>   (*F. Q.*, III, iv, 11.)

After Timias had fallen under Belphoebe's displeasure he never laughed again:

> But alwaies wept and wailed night and day,
> As blasted bloosme through heat doth languish
>   and decay (*F. Q.*, IV, viii, 2).

A turtle-dove joined her lament to his:

> With that he forth would poure so plenteous teares,
> And beat his breast unworthy of such blame,
> And knocke his head, and rend his rugged heares,
> That could have perst the hearts of tigres and of
>   beares (*F. Q.*, IV, viii, 4).

Marinell, suffering the pangs of love for Florimell, could neither eat nor sleep,

> But pyn'd, and mourn'd, and languisht,
>   and alone did weepe (*F. Q.*, IV, xii, 19).

Sir Scudamour, "inly groning deepe and sighing oft," prays for help in the Temple of Venus (*F. Q.*, IV, x, 48). Mirabella was beloved of many, but—

What cared she, who sighed for her sore,
Or who did wayle or watch the weary night.
(F. Q., VI, vii, 30.)[63]

Many a shepherd loved Pastorella,

and with sweet pleasing payns
Full many a night for her did sigh and grone.
(F. Q., VI, ix, 10.)[64]

The lover grows pale, trembles, and even suffers a temporary paralysis of his faculties. In the *Romance of the Rose* the God of Love says that various troubles

Makith lovers withouten ony wene
Under her clothes pale and lene.[65]
(vv. 2685–2686.)

In the January eclogue of the *Shepheardes Calender* the poet says of the lover:

All as the sheepe, such was the shepeheardes looke,
For pale and wanne he was, (alas the while!)
May seeme he lovd, or els some care he tooke.
(vv. 7–9.)

Prince Arthur describes his vision of the Faerie Queene and tells of his love for her:

Thus as he spake, his visage wexed pale,
And chaunge of hew great passion did bewray.
(F. Q., I, ix, 16.)

When Sir Artegall saw the face of Britomart, he fell at her feet:

---

[63] Cf. her statement to Prince Arthur:
Full many a one for me deepe groand and sight.
(F. Q., VI, viii, 20.)

[64] It should be noted that the bellows in the House of Care, where the lovelorn Scudamour spent a wretched night, were "Sighes" (F. Q., IV, v, 38).

[65] The idea is Ovidian:
Palleat omnis amans: hic est color aptus amanti.
(*Ars amatoria*, I, 729.)
Cf. Andreas Capellanus, *De Amore*, ed. by Trojel, p. 310; *Romance of Flamenca*, Appel, *Prov. Chrest.*, p. 24, vv. 10–13; Chaucer, *The Book of the Duchesse*, v. 1215; and the *Court of Love*, v. 958.

> Whilest trembling horrour did his sense assayle,
> And made ech member quake and manly hart to quayle.
> (*F. Q.*, IV, vi, 22.)[66]

He was temporarily struck dumb before her.[67] Paridell swoons for love of Hellenore (*F. Q.*, III, x, 7).[68]

The logical result of the lover's afflictions is illness. Love becomes a disease[69]—a malady generally incurable by ordinary treatment. In Chrétien's *Cligés* Alexander soliloquizes on his love for Soredamors:

> Je sant le mien mal si grevain
> Que ja n'an avrai garison
> Par mecine ne par poison
> Ne par herbe ne par racine.[70]
> (vv. 646-649.)

In the *Faerie Queene* Britomart pronounces love an ulcerated wound that

> Now rancleth in this same fraile fleshly mould,
> That all mine entrails flow with poisnous gore,
> And th' ulcer groweth daily more and more;
> Ne can my ronning sore finde remedie,
> Other then my hard fortune to deplore,
> And languish as the leafe faln from the tree,
> Till death make one end of my daies and miseree.
> (*F. Q.*, III, ii, 39.)

---

[66] In Chrétien's *Cligés* the queen observes Alexander and Soredamors,
> Et voit l'un et l'autre sovant
> Descolorer et anpalir
> Et sospirer et tressalir (vv. 542-544).

Cf. William IX of Poitou, Appel, *Prov. Chrest.*, p. 52, vv. 31-34. Andreas Capellanus says, further, that the sudden appearance of the beloved causes a violent palpitation of the lover's heart. See *De Amore*, ed. by Trojel, p. 311, and cf. *F. Q.*, IV, vi, 29, where it is said of Britomart on the occasion of her first meeting with her knight that,
> Soone as she heard the name of Artegall,
> Her hart did leape, and all her hart-strings tremble.

[67] Dr. Long (*Elizabethan Courtly Love*, Ch. II) calls attention to the parallel between this situation and that of Chrétien's Lancelot before Guenevere. Cf. *Flamenca*, vv. 18-21, and Petrarch, Sonetto CX: "Perseguendomi Amor."

[68] Amadis of Gaul swooned on receiving word that Oriana had renounced him. Cf. *Romance of the Rose*, vv. 1735-1736.

[69] Cf. Lowes, J. L., "The Loveres Maladye of Hereos," in *Mod. Phil.*, vol. 11, pp. 491 ff.

[70] Gower (*Confessio Amantis*, III, 2217-2218) speaks of
> The wofull peine of loves maladie,
> Ayein the which mai no phisique availe.

Cf. *Romance of the Rose*, vv. 2643-2644; Guillaume de Machaut, *Dit du Vergier*, *Œuvres*, ed. by P. Tarbé, p. 20; and *De Venus la Deesse d'Amor*, 117, where love causes bleeding at the nose.

Her nurse tries charms but in vain; so

> That through long languor and hart-burning brame
> She shortly like a pyned ghost became,
> Which long hath waited by the Stygian strond.
>
> (*F. Q.,* III, ii, 52.)

Since she can find neither herbes, charms, nor counsel, which is "choisest med'cine for sick harts reliefe" (*F. Q.,* III, iii, 5), old Glauce takes the "sicke damosell" to Merlin. The magician suggests that Britomart needs "leach-crafte" rather than magic, but the nurse replies that her daughter's "deepe engraffed ill" is beyond "any leaches skill" (*F. Q.,* III, iii, 17–18). Merlin finally diagnoses the case as love for Artegall, her destined lord.

Under the skillful treatment of Belphoebe the young squire, Timias, grew better of his wounds, but his "hart woxe sore, and health decayd," so that the more she applied plasters to his wound,

> So still his malady the more increast.
>
> (*F. Q.,* III, v, 43.)

He was finally forced to yield himself to the illness,

> Which as a victor proud, gan ransack fast
> His inward partes, and all his entrayles waste,
> That neither blood in face nor life in hart
> It left, but both did quite drye up and blast;
> As percing levin, which the inner part
> Of every thing consumes and calcineth by art.
>
> (*F. Q.,* III, v, 48.)

The Knight Marinell so pined for love of Florimell,

> That in short space his wonted chearefull hew
> Gan fade, and lively spirits deaded quight:
> His cheeke bones raw, and eie-pits hollow grew,
> And brawney armes had lost their knowen might,
> That nothing like himselfe he seem'd in sight.
> Ere long so weake of limbe, and sicke of love
> He woxe, that lenger he note stand upright,

> But to his bed was brought, and layd above,
> Like ruefull ghost, unable once to stirre or move.
>   (*F. Q.*, IV, xii, 20.)[71]

His mother sought to find

> The secret cause and nature of his teene,
> Whereby she might apply some medicine.
>   (*F. Q.*, IV, xii, 21.)

But she was unsuccessful:

> Nought could she read the roote of his disease,
> Ne weene what mister maladie it is,
> Whereby to seeke some meanes it to appease.
>   (*F. Q.*, IV, xii, 22.)

In the belief that an old wound had not thoroughly healed she had Tryphon re-examine her son.   The old physician declared, however, that the trouble was not due to an old sore,

> But that it was some other maladie,
> Or griefe unknowne, which he could not discerne:
> So left he her withouten remedie.
>   (*F. Q.*, IV, xii, 24.)

The correct diagnosis was finally given by Apollo, "king of leaches."

In *Amoretti* 50 Spenser reasons that, since love attacks the heart with particular violence, the only source of permanent relief is the lady herself—

> Long languishing in double malady,
> Of my harts wound and of my bodies griefe,
> There came to me a leach, that would apply
> Fit medicines for my bodies best reliefe.
> Vayne man! (quod I) that hast but little
>   priefe
> In deep discovery of the mynds disease,
> Is not the hart of all the body chiefe,
> And rules the members as it selfe doth please?

---

[71] Quoted in part by Lowes, *Mod. Phil.*, vol. 11, 1914, p. 544.   With Spenser's description of the love-sick Marinell cf. the same scholar's quotations from Chaucer, *Knight's Tale*, A 1361–76; and from Boccaccio, *La Teseide*, Lib. IV, sts. 26–29. See Lowes, *op. cit.*, pp. 491–492 and 525.

> Then with some cordialls seeke first to appease
> The inward languour of my wounded hart,
> And then my body shall have shortly ease:
> But such sweet cordialls passe physitions art.
> Then, my lyfes leach, doe you your skill reveale,
> And with one salve both hart and body heale.[72]

In view of the conventional recognition of love as a disease which attacks both mind and body, it is not inappropriate that Spenser has included Infirmity among the attendants of the God of Love in the Masque of Cupid (*F. Q.*, III, xii, 25).

Deprived of his lady's grace the lover has left only one avenue of relief—death. This is the final effect of love.[73]

In the August eclogue of the *Shepheardes Calender* the lover retires in despair to the forest and says:

> Here will I dwell apart
> In gastfull grave therefore, till my last sleepe
> Doe close mine eyes (vv. 169–171).

In the December eclogue he asks himself:

> Why livest thou stil, and yet hast thy
> deathes wound?
> Why dyest thou stil, and yet alive art
> founde? (vv. 95–96).

In *Colin Clouts Come Home Again* Colin says:

> And ye, my fellow shepheardes, which do see
> And beare the languors of my too long dying,

---

[72] The lady is usually appealed to as the sick lover's last hope. Cf. Caulier's *L'Hospital d'Amours,* where the lover is brought to the infirmary provided for love-patients and is there attended by Hope, Pity, and others; but continues to languish until finally cured by a kiss from his lady.

[73] Schrötter (*Ovid und die Troubadours,* p. 76) remarks:
> Die Beteuerung, dass man vor Sehnsucht sterbe, wird von Ovid vorgeschrieben und gilt bei ihm wie bei den Troubadours als Ausdruck der höchsten, grenzenlosen Liebe.

The lover in Caulier's *L'Hospital d'Amours* visits the cemetery:
> En ce cimitiere gisoient
> Les vrais & loyaulx amoureux,
> Leurs epitaphes devisoient
> Leurs noms. Si recongneuz entre eulx
> Tristan le Chevalier trespreux,
> Le quel mourut de desconfort,
> Lancelot du Lac, & tous ceulx
> Qui aymerent iusqu'à la mort.

(*Œuvres de Chartier,* ed. by Du Chesne, p. 732.)

Unto the world for ever witnesse bee,
That hers I die (vv. 947–950).

In *Amoretti* 2 the poet bids his "unquiet thought" seek grace of his lady:

Which if she graunt, then live, and my love cherish,
If not, die soone, and I with thee will perish.[74]

In the *Hymne in Honour of Love* the lover complains to the God of Love:

Certes small glory doest thou winne hereby,
To let her live thus free, and me to dy.
(vv. 153–154.)

Britomart, in love with Artegall, sees no end to her misery save in death (*F. Q.*, III, ii, 39). So she complains to her nurse:

But wicked fortune mine, though minde be good,
Can have no end, nor hope of my desire,
But feed on shadowes, whiles I die for food,
And like a shadow wexe, whiles with entire
Affection I doe languish and expire.
(*F. Q.*, III, ii, 44.)

Later, her conversation with the Redcross Knight concerning Artegall so increases her affliction,

That nought but death her dolour mote depart.
(*F. Q.*, III, iv, 6.)

Though the young knight Marinell avoided the love of ladies,

Yet many ladies fayre did oft complaine
That they for love of him would algates dy.
(*F. Q.*, III, iv, 26.)[75]

---

[74] Cf. the plea of the lover in the M. E. *Court of Love*:
The frosty grave and cold must be my bedde,
Without ye list your grace and mercy shewe,
Deth with his axe so faste on me doth hewe.
(vv. 978–980.)
[75] In Chrétien's *Cligés* Fenice suffers mortal pangs on account of her absent lover:
Morte sui, quant celui ne voi,
Qui de mon cuer m'a desrobee (vv. 4456–4457).

Paridell wept and wailed for love of Hellenore,

> Saying, but if she mercie would him give,
> That he mote algates dye, yet did his death forgive.
> (F. Q., III, x, 7.)[76]

To Britomart's proffer of aid in the search for the lost Amoret the hopeless Scudamour replies:

> O spare thy happy daies, and them apply
> To better boot, but let me die, that ought;
> More is more losse: one is enough to dy.
> (F. Q., III, xi, 19.)

As a result of the cruel disdain of Mirabella,

> Many a wretch, for want of remedie,
> Did languish long in life consuming smart,
> And at the last through dreary dolour die.
> (F. Q., VI, vii, 31.)

So when Cupid held his court and called the roll of his followers, it was found

> That many there were missing, which were ded.
> (F. Q., VI, vii, 33.)

Evidence showed that the missing lovers had been betrayed,

> And murdred cruelly by a rebellious mayd.
> (F. Q., VI, vii, 34.)

This maid—Mirabella—later confessed to Prince Arthur that in her youth many a knight had sighed for her love,

> And to the dore of death for sorrow drew.
> (F. Q., VI, viii, 20.)

---

[76] Cf. Chrétien de Troyes, Yvain, vv. 6510–6516. The typical courtly lover even glories in the thought of such a death. Says Folquet de Romans (Raynouard, Lexique roman, vol. I, p. 491):

> Qu'anc homs non fes tan bella mort
> Com ieu farai, s'ieu mort per vos,
> Per qu'en dei esser mout joios.

In rare instances the lover commits suicide. In the first book of the *Faerie Queene* two disappointed lovers, Sir Trevisan and Sir Terwin, encounter Despair, who, after plucking from them all hope and urging them to die, ends by giving Sir Terwin a "rusty knife":

> With which sad instrument of hasty death,
> That wofull lover, loathing lenger light,
> A wyde way made to let forth living breath.[77]
> (*F. Q.*, I, ix, 30.)

Spenser doubtless designed to allegorize this conventional association of love and death when he included Death among the personified masquers who follow in Cupid's train through the halls of the House of Busirane (*F. Q.*, III, xii, 25).

[77] Cf. the *De Venus la Deesse d'Amor*, 57, where the lover declares that only the lack of a sword prevents his taking his own life.

III

THE COURTLY SYSTEM IN SPENSER: LAWS OF LOVE

As the relations between mediaeval lover and lady were conventionalized and gradually reduced to a hard and fast system, there grew up rules and regulations designed to set forth the theory and practice of courtly love-making. To these regulations the lover was required scrupulously to conform.

Thus the lover in the *Romance of the Rose* asks the God of Love to give him instructions for his own guidance.[1] Laws were needed not only to guide the lover but also to restrain the lady. In justifying the punishment of Mirabella's cruelty to lovers Prince Arthur says that such procedure may be necessary to safeguard Cupid's realm:

> For were no law in love, but all that lust
> Might them oppresse, and painefully turmoile,
> His kingdome would continue but a while.
> (*F. Q.*, VI, viii, 23.)

Although the lady as well as the lover is subject to Love's sovereignty and amenable to certain statutes, it is nevertheless true that extant codes such as those of Andreas Capellanus and of the *Court of Love* were framed primarily for the lover.[2] It is chiefly from this point of view, therefore, that we shall study the influence of the general laws as well as of particular codes of love upon Spenser. And, though Spenser has nowhere embodied in his work a formal code, the influence of such laws upon his lovers will be found to be considerable. For courtly canons regulate the conduct of his knights and ladies and largely determine their philosophy of love.

---

[1] A sire for Goddis love seid I
Er ye passe hens ententyfly
Youre comaundementis to me ye say
And I shall kepe hem if I may (vv. 2135–2138).

[2] In the *Court of Love* (vv. 519 ff.) the lover at the court of Venus is denied a knowledge of the statutes for ladies. They are kept secret on orders from the goddess herself.

The first general law to be considered is that which excludes the *vilain* from the realm of courtly love and limits its privileges to the *cortois*. Contrasting the two classes is a favorite pastime of mediaeval writers. The wide gulf separating the noble from the peasant is dwelt upon.[3] The latter, barred by birth from a knowledge of the usages of courtly society, is incapable of love-making because he is ignorant of the lover's character and accomplishments. Later, a supplementary rule applies the criterion of conduct. He is *cortois* who practices *cortoisie* and he is *vilain* who does *vilenie*.[4]

In Spenser the moral and the class distinctions harmonize. The baseborn "carle" betrays his mean origin in his vulgar conduct, while the high-born cavalier everywhere proclaims his gentle birth in his knightly deeds. The friend of Leicester and Sidney, who took his name from "an house of auncient fame" does not contemplate the *vilain* as a class as having part or lot in courtly love.[5] The aim of the *Faerie Queene* is "to fashion a gentleman or noble person in vertuous and gentle

---

[3] Galpin, S. L., *Cortois and Vilain*, New Haven, 1905, pp. 6 ff.

[4] Galpin, *op. cit.*, pp. 10 ff.

[5] There are two points which may weaken, though I scarcely think they will render untenable, the view here expressed:

(1) Dr. Long (*Elizabethan Courtly Love*, Ch. II) observes that an exception to the law in the Elizabethan Age is the pastoral convention. Technically, the law would exclude the rustic shepherd, and thus pure pastoralism would nullify the statute. But, owing to the artificiality of the Elizabethan pastoral in general and the Spenserian pastoral in particular, this difficulty is more apparent than real. It need hardly be pointed out that Spenser's pastoral lovers are courtiers thinly disguised in shepherds' weeds and transplanted to a rural setting. Their ideas, language, and manners remain practically unchanged. So far as the *Shepheardes Calender* is concerned, this fact is further emphasized by the transparent nature of the personal and political allegory of the poem. Colin is Spenser himself and Rosalind, as E. K. is careful to tell us in the gloss to the April eclogue, "is a gentlewoman of no meane house, nor endewed with anye vulgare and common gifts both of nature and manners." He compares her to Petrarch's Laura. In *Colin Clouts Come Home Again* (vv. 931–938) the lover says that she is far superior to the common shepherdess. Sir Calidore's wooing of Pastorella can not be cited as a violation of the spirit of the law; for from the beginning she is treated by the other shepherds as a superior being (*F. Q.*, VI, ix, 9), and in the end she is shown to be of noble birth (*F. Q.*, VI, xii, 3–22).

(2) As pictured on the walls in the House of Busirane,
Kings, queenes, lords, ladies, knights, and
damsels gent
Were heap'd together with the vulgar sort,
And mingled with the raskall rablement,
Without respect of person or of port,
To shew Dan Cupids powre and great effort.
(*F. Q.*, III, xi, 46.)

This is in substantial agreement with the observation of Alanus de Insulis (*De Planctu Naturae*, trans. of Moffat, p. 47) that love is a thing which "the purple of the king feels, and which does not pass by the toga of a beggar." All that can be said is that in courtly literature such democratic doctrine is rare, and is therefore to be regarded rather as the exception than as the rule.

discipline.[6]   Here is no thought of the common herd. The apostrophe that begins the ninth canto of Book III is, therefore, significant:

> Redoubted knights, and honorable dames,
> To whom I levell all my labours end.[7]

With reference to Britomart's susceptibility to love, Spenser says:

> But as it falleth, in the gentlest harts
> Imperious Love hath highest set his throne.
> <div align="right">(<i>F. Q.</i>, III, ii, 23.)[8]</div>

In giving the lineage of Sir Satyrane the poet says that his mother, the lady Thyamis, was wedded

> To Therion, a loose unruly swayne,
> Who had more joy to raunge the forrest wyde,
> And chase the salvage beast with busie payne,
> Then serve his ladies love, and waste in
>   pleasures vayne (<i>F. Q.</i>, I, vi, 21).

As the choice of the term "swayne" indicates, Therion was of so low origin and hence so ignorant of the service due to ladies that he was supplanted by a satyr, the latter becoming the father of Sir Satyrane.

Coarse exhibitions of lust, especially when accompanied with attempted violence, are clear marks of the *vilain*. While Florimell was staying at the house of a witch, the latter's son, "a chorle,"

---

[6] *Works,* ed. by Dodge, p. 136.

[7] Cf. the Prologue to Rolland's *Court of Venus,* where the author advises his book to seek favor of the nobility:
> For Gentilmen can richt well thee considder.
> For commoun folk will call the lawit and lidder.
> Thy self present to nobill men and gude,
> And fle the sect of Rurall folke and rude (vv. 325–328).

Text edited by Rev. Walter Gregor for Scottish Text Society, vol. III, Edinburgh, 1884.

[8] In the *Romance of the Rose* the God of Love offers to let the lover kiss his mouth, Which to no vilayn was never couthe
> For curteis and of fair manere
> Well taught and full of gentilnesse
> He must ben that shall me kysse.
> (vv. 2000, 2004–2006.)

> through her so kind
> And courteise use, conceiv'd affection bace,
> And cast to love her in his brutish mind,
> No love, but brutish lust, that was so
> beastly tind (*F. Q.,* III, vii, 15).[9]

The fisherman in whose boat she later took refuge attempted to violate her honour, for he was one "that never good nor maners knew" (*F. Q.,* III, viii, 26).

Braggadochio brazenly assumed to be a knight but betrayed his *vilain* nature when, ravished with Belphoebe's beauty, he

> Gan burne in filthy lust, and, leaping light,
> Thought in his bastard armes her to embrace.
> (*F. Q.,* II, iii, 42.)

Hence Spenser calls him a "pesaunt." The impostor's horse recognizes his master's low breeding from his awkwardness in riding. This fact leads Spenser to point out the contrast between the *cortois* and the *vilain* in this as in other respects:

> In brave poursuitt of honourable deed,
> There is I know not what great difference
> Betweene the vulgar and the noble seed,
> Which unto things of valorous pretence
> Seemes to be borne by native influence;
> As feates of armes, and love to entertaine;
> But chiefly skill to ride seemes a science
> Proper to gentle blood: some others faine
> To menage steeds, as did this vaunter;
> but in vaine (*F. Q.,* II, iv, 1).

As regards skill in love the contrast between noble and peasant is equally sharp. This difference is illustrated in the wooing of Pastorella by Sir Calidore and Coridon. The shepherd shows his *vilain* birth when he flees a tiger and leaves Pastorella to be rescued by Sir Calidore; whom thenceforth the maiden more and more "affects," leaving Coridon as one

> Fit to keepe sheepe, unfit for loves content.
> (*F. Q.,* VI, x, 37.)

In the final test blood tells and as like seeks like Pastorella and Sir Calidore are instinctively drawn together, while the

---

[9] In Huon de Mery's *Le Tornoiement de L'Antéchrist* (ed. by Tarbé, p. 32) the author warns the reader against confounding Love and Fornication:
> Amor n'a pas si vilain non.
> Non; qu'Amor naist de Cortoisie.

maiden's earlier antipathy to Coridon is explained and justified.
The shepherd fails utterly to evince the qualities of the courtly
lover. He is to be regarded not so much a rival as a foil to the
knight, who everywhere obeys the injunction of Andreas
Capellanus:

> In omnibus urbanum te constituas et curialem.[10]

The law not only eliminates the *vilain* but also prohibits all
vilenie.[11] With the development of a moral ideal *vilenie*
becomes associated with vice and *cortoisie* with virtue. Spenser
says that true love is "that sweete fit" that "choseth Vertue for
his dearest dame" (*F. Q.,* III, iii, 1).[12] Hence his true knights
are careful of their conduct. By Archimago's magic a wicked
dream and a counterfeit Una are sent at night to tempt the Redcross Knight to evil, but he successfully resists their allurements
(*F. Q.,* I, i, 47–55). To have yielded would have been both
vilenie and sin. The young squire Timias, though suffering the
pangs of love for Belphoebe, would not reveal his heart,

> But rather chose to dye for sorrow great
> Then with dishonorable termes her to entreat.
> > (*F. Q.,* III, v, 49.)

The knightly lover must not only abstain from base conduct
himself, but he must also prevent it in others:

> For he me seemes most fit the faire to serve,
> That can her best defend from villenie.
> > (*F. Q.,* IV, v, 1.)

A second general law demands of the courtly lover absolute
loyalty both to the beloved and to the God of Love.[13] Unswerv-

---

[10] *De Amore,* Trojel's ed., p. 106.

[11] In *Le Roman de la Rose* this is the first commandment given to the lover by the
God of Love. See vv. 2067–2073 and cf. M. E. version, vv. 2199–2202.

[12] Cf. Andreas Capellanus:
> Probitas sola quemque dignum facit amore.
> > (*De Amore,* Trojel's ed. p. 311.)

In Lydgate's *Temple of Glas* Venus says to the lover:
> And al vertues biseli þou sue,
> Vices eschew, for þe love of oon.
> > (vv. 1180–1181.)

[13] The thrid statut was clerely write also
> Withouten chaunge to live and dye the same,
> Non other love to take, for wele ne wo,
> For brind delyt, for ernest nor for game.
> > (*Court of Love,* vv. 316–319.)

ing loyalty is held throughout the world of chivalry to be a virtue essential to knighthood. Spenser indicates in the invocation to the first book of the *Faerie Queene* that this principle is to govern the relations of his ideal knights and ladies:

> Fierce warres and faithful loves shall moralize my song.

Of the Redcross Knight he says:

> Right faithfull true he was in deede and word.
> (F. Q., I, i, 2.)

The Knight slew Sansfoy, the incarnation of disloyalty (*F. Q.,* I, ii, 19). Later, deceived by Archimago's magic into believing Una false to him, he rashly fled from her. But when his lady's fidelity and devotion had been vindicated, remorse for his faithless conduct drove him to attempt suicide in the Cave of Despair (*F. Q.,* I, ix, 51).

> For unto knight there is no greater shame,
> Then lightnesse and inconstancie in love:
> That doth this Redcrosse Knights ensample
> plainly prove (F. Q., I, iv, 1).

Rescued by the faithful Una he remained loyal to the end. Even after his separation from his lady and return to court he kept his vows, for in the third book of the *Faerie Queene* he was attacked by six knights from Castle Joyous because he refused to renounce his lady and love the Lady of Delight. During the combat Britomart arrived on the scene and after stopping the fray espoused the side of the Redcross Knight:

> For knight to leave his lady were great shame,
> That faithful is, and better were to dy.
> All losse is lesse, and lesse the infamy,
> Then losse of love to him that loves but one.
> (F. Q., III, i, 25.)

Britomart and Artegall were loyal to each other. The poet urges all ladies to profit by the example of her

> That was as trew in love as turtle to her make.
> (*F. Q.*, III, xi, 2.)[14]

Britomart demonstrated her loyalty by going to the rescue of Artegall, in spite of her jealous fears, when she learned of his bondage to Radigund (*F. Q.*, V, vi, 17–18). Artegall did, indeed, show himself friendly to Clarinda in the hope of gaining his freedom:

> Yet never meant he in his noble mind,
> To his owne absent love to be untrew.
> (*F. Q.*, V, v, 56.)

For, notwithstanding the efforts of the Amazons to entrap him, he behaved himself so well that

> To his owne love his loialtie he saved.
> (*F. Q.*, V, vi, 2.)

For, as he said to another,

> Dearer is love then life, and fame then gold;
> But dearer then them both your faith once plighted hold.
> (*F. Q.*, V, xi, 63.)

The fair Florimell was loved of many a knight, but she loved Marinell alone. When rumour said that he had been slain, she left the court,

> And vowed never to returne againe,
> Till him alive or dead she did invent.
> (*F. Q.*, III, v, 10.)

The god Proteus sought her love in vain. He threw her into a dungeon, but

---

[14] The dove is the proverbial representative of constancy in love. Spenser uses the bird to bring about a reconciliation between Timias and Belphoebe after their estrangement on account of Amoret (*F. Q.*, IV, viii, 1 ff.). In Chaucer's *Parlement of Foules* the turtle dove takes a firm stand for loyalty in love:
> Nay, God forbede a lover shulde chaunge!
> Thogh that his lady evermore be straunge,
> Yet let him serve hir ever, til he be deed.
See Dodd, *Courtly Love in Chaucer and Gower*, pp. 125 ff.

> Eternall thraldome was to her more liefe,
> Then losse of chastitie, or chaunge of love:
> Dye had she rather in tormenting griefe,
> Then any should of falsenesse her reprove,
> Or loosenes, that she lightly did remove.
>
> (*F. Q.*, III, viii, 42.)

Her chastity in love was further shown by the character of the girdle which she wore:

> That girdle gave the vertue of chaste love
> And wivehood true to all that did it beare.
>
> (*F. Q.*, IV, v, 3.)[15]

Her faithfulness was rewarded by her union with Marinell.

Equally notable is the constancy of Amoret. Introduced at court, she was beloved of many knights; but she gave her love to only one, Sir Scudamour,

> To whom her loving hart she linked fast
> In faithfull love, t'abide for evermore.
>
> (*F. Q.*, III, vi, 53.)

All the magic of Busirane failed to move her "stedfast hart" (*F. Q.*, III, xii, 31). After seven months of torture she was released by Britomart and restored to Scudamour, who declared that he now counted as naught all his sufferings,

> Since of my love at length I rest assured,
> That to disloyalty she will not be allured.
>
> (*F. Q.*, IV, x, 2.)

Sir Guyon refused Mammon's offer of the fair Philotime on the ground that he was unworthy of such a match, but added:

> And were I not, yet is my trouth yplight,
> And love avowd to other lady late,
> That to remove the same I have no might:
> To chaunge love causelesse is reproch
> to warlike knight (*F. Q.*, II, vii, 50).

---

[15] The same girdle proved Amoret chaste towards Scudamour (*F. Q.*, IV, v, 19). The fate of the unchaste lover is seen in the case of Locrine (*F. Q.*, II, x, 17–19). The law of chastity in love is stated concisely by Andreas Capellanus:
Castitatem servare debes amanti.
(*De Amore*, Trojel's ed., p. 106.)
Cf. Chrétien's *Lancelot*, vv. 1207–1292.

Thus it ever was in antiquity, says the poet, for—

> Then loyall love had royall regiment,
> And each unto his lust did make a lawe,
> From all forbidden things his liking to
>   withdraw (*F. Q.,* IV, viii, 30).

For the bonds of love are sacred:

> There Pride dare not approch,
>   nor Discord spill
> The league twixt them that loyal
>   love hath bound (*Amoretti,* 65).

It is clear that the law does not countenance divided affection,

> For love can not endure a paragone.[16]
>   (*Hymne in Honour of Love,* v. 251.)

Of Astrophel Spenser says:

> For one alone he cared, for one he sight,
> His lifes desire, and his deare loves
>   delight (vv. 53–54).

This one was Stella:

> Her he did love, her he alone did honor,
> His thoughts, his rimes, his songs were
>   all upon her (vv. 59–60).[17]

Finally, the lover is bound to be loyal to the God of Love,

> For Love is lord of truth and loialtie.[18]
>   (*Hymne in Honour of Love,* v. 176.)

---

[16] See *Romance of the Rose,* vv. 2361–2366.

[17] Yet many knights may love one lady or *vice versa:*
> Unam feminam nil prohibet a duobus amari et a duabus mulieribus unum.
>   (Andreas Capellanus, *De Amore,* Trojel's ed., p. 312.)
Many at the court of the Faerie Queene loved Amoret (*F. Q.,* III, vi, 52). Florimell was beloved by many knights (*F. Q.,* IV, ii, 26). Many combats were fought for the hand of Canace (*F. Q.,* IV, ii, 35–37).

[18] The *first* statut that on the boke was spred,
> Was, To be true in thought and dedes all
> Unto the King of Love, the Lord ryall.
>   (*Court of Love,* vv. 304–306.)

Yet Spenser recognizes that Disloyalty lurks among Cupid's followers, for it appears personified in the Masque of Cupid (*F. Q.,* III, xii, 25).

The code of courtly love enjoined secrecy. The law originated in the fear of detection. The Ovidian lover stood in constant dread of a jealous husband. Thence arose an elaborate system of communication by sign.[19]   The intrigue of Paridell and Hellenore was carried on quite in this spirit (*F. Q.,* III, ix, 27–31). Paridell sat on the husband's blind side and thus "sent close messages of love to her at will." With "speaking lookes,[20] that close embassage bore," he "told his secret care." By this and other

> close signes they secret way did make
> Unto their wils, and one eies watch escape.

Thus flattering her "ever privily," the lover so adroitly stole away the heart of Hellenore,

> That Cupid selfe, it seeing, close did smyle,
> . . . .
> And bad that none their joyous treason should reveale.
> (*F. Q.,* III, x, 5.)

Under the god's approving glance Paridell bore himself so well

> that none espyde
> His secret drift, till he her layd abord.
> (*F. Q.,* III, x, 6.)

Under the feudal system the vassal was bound to keep secret the affairs of his lord. The lover, as the vassal of his lady, felt the same obligation.[21]   Hence the law was quickly established in courtly poetry and soon became generally recognized

---

[19] See *Amores,* I, iv.

[20] Cf. *F. Q.,* I, iv, 25, where Lechery "learned had to love with secret lookes."

[21] Wechssler, *Frauendienst und Vassallität, in Zeit. f. fr. Sp. u. Lit.,* vol. 24, p. 169 (footnote).

in mediaeval literature.[22]   As in Provence, however, so in the
Elizabethan age the secrecy was largely, if not purely, conventional.   The use of the *senhal* by the troubadours did, indeed,
conceal the name of the lady; but it is doubtful whether it concealed her identity, for the main purpose of the lover's addresses was to increase the fame of his mistress.   There was
never any question as to who Sidney's Stella was.   The same
thing may be said of Spenser's Rosalind.   It is true that we
do not know her identity today, but it was evidently known to
Spenser's friends.[23]   Other references to the law in the poet's
work are also of a conventional nature.   In *Astrophel* the
shepherds are wont to "plain" their loves' "concealed smart"
(v. 2).   In *Amoretti* 34 the lover wanders comfortless,

> In secret sorrow and sad pensivenesse.

In Book IV of the *Faerie Queene* Prince Arthur, after rescuing
the Squire of Low Degree, pursued his original quest of Glori-
ana, for his mind travailed,

> as with chylde
> Of his old love, conceav'd in secret brest.
> (*F. Q.,* IV, ix, 17.)

Marinell hid his passion even from his mother:

> Least did she thinke, that which he most
>   concealed,
> That love it was, which in his hart
>   lay unrevealed (*F. Q.,* IV, xii, 22).

Sir Calidore was friendly to Coridon,

---

[22] Qui non zelat, amare non potest.
                (Andreas Capellanus, *De Amore,* Trojel's ed. p. 310.)
    In Chrétien's *Cligés,* when Alexander learned that Soredamors had woven in his golden
shirt some locks of her hair,
                Mout an feit tote nuit grant joie,
                Meis bien se garde qu'an nel voie.
                        (vv. 1635–1636.)
    See also Wechssler, *op. cit.,* p. 171; Diez, *Poesie der Troubadours,* pp. 129 ff.; *Ro-
mance of the Rose,* vv. 2391–2394; and the *Court of Love,* vv. 309–311.
    [23] See the oft-quoted remark of E. K. in the gloss to the April eclogue of the *Shep-
heardes Calender.* According to this authority, it was "well knowen" that she was of a
distinguished family.

> That by his fellowship he colour might
> Both his estate and love from skill of
> any wight (*F. Q.*, VI, x, 37).

Britomart hid her love of Artegall under a show of mortal hatred (*F. Q.*, III, ii, 8 ff.). Radigund long concealed her love from Artegall (*F. Q.*, V, v, 27).[24]

The exigencies of courtly love-making demanded discretion. The conditions that necessitated secrecy required also extreme caution and prudence on the part of both lover and lady. This was necessary in order that lovers might escape detection and circumvent tattlers, of whom mediaeval courtly poets continually complain and of whom they were ever wary. It was this consideration which led Andreas Capellanus to warn lovers against having many confidants in love.[25]

Spenser's Britomart revealed her love to only one—her faithful nurse Glauce, and then only after much coaxing (*F. Q.*, III, ii, 30 ff.). Radigund confided only in her maid Clarinda (*F. Q.*, V, v, 29–30).[26] Prince Arthur and Amoret rode many miles together,

> To seeke their loves dispersed diversly,
> Yet neither showed to other their hearts
> privity (*F. Q.*, IV, ix, 19).

It was care for her honor that made Canace discreet:

> Full many lords and many knights her loved,
> Yet she to none of them her liking lent,
> Ne ever was with fond affection moved,
> But rul'd her thoughts with goodly governement,
> For dread of blame and honours blemishment;

---

[24] Fenice loves Cligés,
  Meis bien li cele et bien le noie,
  Se nus li demande qu' ele a.
    (*Cligés*, vv. 3000–3001.)

[25] Amoris tui secretarios noli plures habere.
    (*De Amore*, ed. by Trojel, p. 106.)

[26] Hence the precept—doubtless culled from Ovid—which urges the lover to cultivate the good-will of his lady's maid:
  Yit with o thing I thee charge
  That it to seye that thou be large
  Unto the mayde that hir doith serve.
    (*Romance of the Rose*, vv. 2695–2697.)

> And eke unto her lookes a law she made,
> That none of them once out of order went,
> But, like to warie centonels well stayd,
> Still watcht on every side, of secret foes
>   affrayd (*F. Q.*, IV, ii, 36).[27]

The less careful lady Priscilla, having fled from her father's
castle and finding herself in the embarrassing role of refugee
in the home of her lover's father,

> gan t' advize,
> How great a hazard she at earst had made
> Of her good fame, and further gan devize,
> How she the blame might salve with
>   coloured disguize (*F. Q.*, VI, iii, 8).

It remained for the wise and courteous Sir Calidore to rescue
the unfortunate lady from her plight. On the other hand, it
was not so much care for the lady's honour as fear of a jealous
husband that made Paridell circumspect in his wooing of
Hellenore:

> When so in open place and commune bord
> He fortun'd her to meet, with commune speach
> He courted her, yet bayted every word,
> That his ungentle hoste n'ote him appeach
> Of vile ungentlenesse, or hospitages breach.
>   (*F. Q.*, III, x, 6.)

Stress is laid upon the principle of humility. The lover's
sense of inferiority makes him humble in his attitude towards
his lady.[28] Timias thought it futile for him, "a meane squyre,
of meeke and lowly place," to aspire to the love of one

---

[27] Cf. the passage in Chrétien's *Cligés* in which Fenice declines to flee to Britain with
Cligés:

> Meis le comandement saint Pol
> Feit buen garder et retenir.
> Qui chastes ne se viaut tenir
> Sainz Pos a feire li ansaigne
> Si sagemant, que il n'an praigne
> Ne cri ne blasme ne reproche (vv. 5324–5329).

[28] The tenth statut was, Egally discern
> By-twene thy lady and thyn abilitee,
> And think, thy-self art never like to yern,
> By right, her mercy, nor of equitee,
> But of her grace and womanly pitee:
> For though thy-self be noble in thy strene,
> A thowsand-fold more nobill is thy quene.
>   (*Court of Love* vv. 365–371.)

"hevenly borne, and of celestiall hew" (*F. Q.*, III, v, 47).
Blandamour wooed the false Florimell

> With humblest suit that he imagine mote.
> > (*F. Q.*, IV, ii, 8.)

Sir Calidore courted Pastorella

> With humble service, and with daily sute.
> > (*F. Q.*, VI, x, 38.)

In *Amoretti* 2 the lover bids his "unquiet thought" fall at his mistress' feet,

> And with meeke humblesse and afflicted mood
> Pardon for thee, and grace for me intreat.[29]

Again, the lover says to his lady:

> To all those happy blessings which ye have,
> With plenteous hand by heaven upon you thrown,
> This one disparagement they to you gave,
> That ye your love lent to so meane a one.
> > (*Amoretti* 66.)

The lover blesses his good fortune and adds:

> But then the more your owne mishap I rew,
> That are so much by so meane love embased.
> > (*Amoretti* 82.)

This humble devotion is intensified to the point of religious worship under the influence of Platonic ideals of love:

> The glorious image of the makers beautie,
> My soverayne saynt, the idoll of my thought,
> Dare not henceforth, above the bounds of dewtie,
> T' accuse of pride, or rashly blame for ought.
> For being, as she is, divinely wrought,
> And of the brood of angels hevenly borne,

---

[29] Cf. Lydgate's *Temple of Glas,* where Venus advises the lover:
> Therfor at ones go in humble wise
> Tofore þi ladi & louli knele adoun
> And in al trouth þi woordis so devyse,
> That she on þe have compassioun (vv. 925-928).

> And with the crew of blessed saynts upbrought,
> Each of which did her with theyr guifts adorne,
> The bud of joy, the blossome of the morne,
> The beame of light, whom mortal eyes admyre,
> What reason is it then but she should scorne
> Base things, that to her love too bold aspire?
> Such heavenly formes ought rather worshipt be,
> Then dare be lov'd by men of meane degree.
>   (*Amoretti* 61.)[30]

For the mediaeval mind the most natural parallel to this relationship was that of the vassal to his lord. The accepted lover became the sworn vassal of his lady.[31] The influence of this convention is clearly observable in Spenser's work. At sight of Britomart's face Artegall dropped upon his knee in sign of submission; whereupon Sir Scudamour remarked:

> Certes, Sir Artegall,
> I joy to see you lout so low on ground,
> And now become to live a ladies thrall,
> That whylome in your minde wont to despise
>   them all (*F. Q.*, IV, vi, 28).

After this Artegall courted Britomart "with meeke service and much suit"; and when ready to set forth on his quest he would not leave her till he had

> Wonne her will to suffer him depart.
>   (*F. Q.*, IV, vi, 43.)

Sir Artegall's subsequent encounter with the Amazon Radigund showed a curious mingling of legal and love vassalage. In the heat of the combat the knight, temporarily unmanned by the Amazon's beauty, threw down his sword and refused to fight any longer. He thus voluntarily yielded himself

---

[30] Dr. Percy W. Long (*Mod. Lang. Rev.*, vol. 3, 1907–1908, pp. 257–267, and vol. 6, 1911, pp. 390–397)—supported in the main contention by Mr. J. C. Smith (*Mod. Lang. Rev.*, vol. 5, 1910, pp. 273–281)—argues very forcibly for Lady Elizabeth Carey rather than Elizabeth Boyle as the mistress for whom the sonnets from the *Amoretti* here discussed were originally composed. If this be true, the purely *courtois* character of the poet's attitude is emphasized.

[31] See Wechssler, *Frauendienst und Vassallität*, in *Zeit. f. franz. Sp. u. Lit.*, vol. 24, pp. 159 ff.

To be her thrall, and service her afford.
>   (*F. Q.,* V, v, 17.)

Tho with her sword on him she flatting strooke,
In signe of true subjection to her powre,
And as her vassall him to thraldome tooke.
>   (*F. Q.,* V, v, 18.)

Radigund in turn became enamoured of her captive but for a while would not yield

To serve the lowly vassall of her might,
And of her servant make her soverayne lord:
So great her pride, that she such basenesse
      much abhord (*F. Q.,* V, v, 27).

In *Colin Clouts Come Home Again* the lover declares himself still the vassal of his early love, Rosalind:

For that my selfe I do professe to be
Vassall to one, whom all my dayes I serve.
>   (vv. 466–467.)

One ever I all vowed hers to bee,
One ever I, and others never none.[32]
>   (vv. 478—479.)

The lover's condition of vassalage is maintained throughout the *Amoretti*:

In vain I seeke and sew to her for grace,
And doe myne humbled hart before her poure.
>   (*Amoretti* 20.)

Let her accept me as her faithful thrall.
>   (*Amoretti* 29.)

The lover does not wish to be free from the pain of love,

But joy, her thrall for ever to remayne,
And yield for pledge my poore captyved hart.
>   (*Amoretti* 42.)

In the *Hymne in Honour of Beautie* the lover prays,

---

[32] With the whole passage cf. Bernart de Ventadorn, in Appel, *Prov. Chrest.,* p. 56, vv. 49-56.

> That I her bounden thrall by her may live,
> And this same life, which first fro me
>   she reaved,
> May owe to her, of whom I it receaved.[33]
>   (vv. 278–280.)

Though accepting the convention of vassalage in love, Spenser apparently declines to sanction the corollary injunction requiring slavish obedience even to the point of suffering shame and dishonor in order to gratify the lady's slightest whim.[34] For after Sir Artegall had been rescued from bondage to Radigund, he determined to proceed upon his first adventure in spite of the fact that he left Britomart "full sad and sorrowfull" (*F. Q.*, V, vii, 44). The knight's resolute adherence to duty is in favorable contrast to the weak conduct of Samson, Hercules, and Antony, who forsook all for love, that made their "mighty hands forget their manlinesse" (*F. Q.*, V, viii, 1–3). Again, Sir Burbon lost his lady to Grandtorto and then laid aside his arms, hoping thereby to "stint all strife" and regain his love. For this Artegall rebuked him:

> Dye rather, then doe ought that mote dishonour
>   yield (*F. Q.*, V, xi, 55).

The loyal lover believes no evil of the beloved,[35] and always defends her honor.[36] Through the magic of Archimago Venus seems to bring to the bed of the sleeping Redcross Knight his lady Una—

---

[33] Cf. *Court of Love*, vv. 876-882.

[34] Dominarum praeceptis in omnibus obediens semper studeas amoris aggregari militiae.
            (Andreas Capellanus, *De Amore*, Trojel's ed., p. 106.)
   In Chrétien's *Lancelot* the hero, for love of the Queen, rides in a cart, regardless of the shame:

> Amors le viaut, et il i saut;
> Que de la honte ne li chaut
> Puis qu' amors le comande et viaut.
>   (vv. 379–381.)
> Doce, por vos perdrai honor et arme et vie.
>   (*Venus la Deesse d'Amor*, 111.)

[35] Construe the best, beleve no tales newe,
        For many a lie is told, that semeth
            full trewe (*Court of Love*, vv. 412–413).

[36] The *fifteenth* statut, use to swere and stare,
        And counterfet a lesing hardely,
        To save thy ladys honour every-where,
        And put thyself to fight for her boldly.
                    (*Court of Love*, vv. 421–424.)

> Her, whom he, waking, evermore did weene
> To be the chastest flowre, that aye did spring
> On earthly braunch (*F. Q.,* I, i, 48).

Though the knight is temporarily led astray, in the end this
faith is justified and the champion of Holiness is happy in the
possession of his lady:

> Ne wicked envy, ne vile gealousy,
> His deare delights were hable to annoy.
>   (*F. Q.,* I, xii, 41.)

In believing Ate's lies about Amoret Sir Scudamour violated
the code and, as a result, landed in the House of Care (*F. Q.,*
IV, v, 30 ff.). *In Colin Clouts Come Home Again* Rosalind
is censured for cruelty to her lover, but the latter quickly
comes to her defense. He reminds the critics that she is of
celestial origin and hence far superior to the common crew
of shepherds:

> Not then to her, that scorned thing so base,
> But to my selfe the blame, that lookt so hie.
>   (vv. 935–936.)

In the *Amoretti,* also, the lover defends his lady from the
charge of being too proud:

> Rudely thou wrongest my deare harts desire,
> In finding fault with her too portly pride.
>   (*Amoretti* 5.)

Courtesy to ladies was a fundamental law of chivalry. The
knightly lover was bound to render every courteous service to
his lady. In *Las Leys d'Amors* we are told that "hom que·s red
enamoratz, no solamen en sos faytz se deu mostrar cortes, ans
o deu far ysshamens en sos digz et en son parlar."[37] Spenser
draws a sharp distinction between his true and his false knights
in this regard. The Redcross Knight replied gently to the overtures of the counterfeit Una sent to his bedside at night and in

---

[37] Appel, *Prov. Chrest.,* p. 198.

embarrassed wonder had her withdraw (*F. Q.,* I, i, 48 ff.). Sir Guyon, as a matter of course, resisted the seductive wiles of Phaedria,

> Yet would not seeme so rude, and thewed ill,
> As to dispise so curteous seeming part,
> That gentle lady did to him impart:
> But fairly tempring fond desire subdewd,
> And ever her desired to depart (*F. Q.,* II, vi, 26).

Sir Artegall saw Britomart blush at thought of granting him her favor,

> Yet durst he not make love so suddenly,
> Ne thinke th' affection of her hart to draw
> From one to other so quite contrary:
> Besides her modest countenance he saw
> So goodly grave, and full of princely aw,
> That it his ranging fancie did refraine,
> And looser thoughts to lawfull bounds
>   withdraw (*F. Q.,* IV, vi, 33).

Spenser contrasts the courtesy and good breeding of Sir Calidore, the champion of courtesy, with the crudeness and boorishness of Coridon. The knight doffed his arms and donning a shepherd's weeds helped Pastorella with her sheep, not only showing no malice towards his jealous rival but even commending the swain and yielding him the place of honor whenever possible. The wisdom of the policy was amply justified:

> For courtesie amongst the rudest breeds
> Good will and favor. So it surely wrought
> With this faire mayd, and in her mynde the seeds
> Of perfect love did sow, that last forth brought
> The fruite of joy and blisse, though long time
>   dearely bought.

> Thus Calidore continu'd there long time,
> To winne the love of the faire Pastorell;
> Which having got, he used without crime
> Or blamefull blot, but menaged so well,
> That he, of all the rest which there did dwell,
> Was favoured and to her grace commended.
>   (*F. Q.,* VI, ix, 45–46.)[38]

---

[38] The advice of Venus to the lover in Lydgate's *Temple of Glas* is:
      Be curteis ay and lowli of þi spech
      To riche and poure (vv. 1166–1167).

With the foregoing contrast the unknightly usage to which the Lady Una is subjected as a captive in the hands of Sansloy:

> Who, by her cleanly garment catching hold,
> Her from her palfrey pluckt, her visage
> to behold (*F. Q.,* I, iii, 40).

In spite of her entreaties,

> He now, lord of the field, his pride to fill,
> With foule reproches and disdaineful spight
> Her vildly entertaines, and, will or nill,
> Beares her away upon his courser light:
> Her prayers nought prevaile; his rage
> is more of might (*F. Q.,* I, iii, 43).

When Florimell greeted Braggadochio with thanks for his supposed championship of her cause, she was rudely rebuffed by this laughing-stock of knighthood and answered with language unbecoming a knight:

> Much did his words the gentle lady quell,
> And turn'd aside for shame to heare what
> he did tell (*F. Q.,* V, iii, 16).

Young Tristram slew a knight for brutal treatment of his own lady and Sir Calidore not only applauded the deed but also knighted the youth on the spot (*F. Q.,* VI, ii, 3 ff.).

The obligation to courtesy rests upon the lady as well as upon the lover:

> What vertue is so fitting for a knight,
> Or for a ladie whom a knight should love,
> As curtesie, to beare themselves aright
> To all of each degree, as doth behove?
> (*F. Q.,* VI, ii, 1.)

The poet warns ladies to beware of abusing the power Love has reposed in them, and adds:

> And as ye soft and tender are by kynde,
> Adornd with goodly gifts of beauties grace,
> So be ye soft and tender eeke in mynde;
> But cruelty and hardnesse from you chace,
> That all your other praises will deface,
> And from you turne the love of men to
> hate (*F. Q.,* VI, viii, 2).

Britomart, mistakenly wooed by Malecasta, felt the obligation to gentle and courteous conduct where affairs of the heart were involved:

> Forthy she would not in discourteise wise
> Scorne the faire offer of good will profest;
> For great rebuke it is, love to despise
> Or rudely sdeigne a gentle harts request.
>> (*F. Q.*, III, i, 55.)[39]

The emphasis placed upon knightly courtesy, courtly entertainment, and love-making, is characteristic as well of the allegory as of the institution of the court of love. Una and the Redcross Knight enter the House of Holiness,

> Where them does meete a francklin faire and free,
> And entertaines with comely courteous glee:
> His name was Zele, that him right well became.
>> (*F. Q.*, I, x, 6.)

In the hall they are received by a squire,

> Of myld demeanure and rare courtesee,
> Right cleanly clad in comely sad attyre;
> In word and deede that shewd great modestee,
> And knew his good to all of each degree,
> Hight Reverence (St. 7).

Una leads her knight to Dame Caelia:

> The auncient dame
> Him goodly greeted in her modest guyse,
> And enterteynd them both, as best became,
> With all the court'sies that she could devyse,
> Ne wanted ought, to shew her bounteous or wise.
>> (St. 11.)

In the same manner Alma, the great lady of the House of Temperance, receives her knightly guests:

> Goodly shee entertaind those noble knights,
> And brought them up into her castle hall;
> Where gentle court and gracious delight

---

[39] It should be noted here that Courtesy is a damsel attendant upon the goddess in the Temple of Venus (*F. Q.*, IV, x, 5).

Cf. also the reflections of Soredamors in Chrétien's *Cligés*:
> Amors voudroit et je le vuel,
> Que sage fusse et sanz orguel
> Et deboneire et acointable,
> Vers toz por un seul amiable (vv. 953–956).

Shee to them made, with mildnesse virginall,
Shewing her selfe both wise and liberall.
There when they rested had a season dew,
They her besought, of favour speciall,
Of that faire castle to affoord them vew:
Shee graunted, and them leading forth, the
        same did shew (*F. Q.*, II, ix, 20).

Britomart and the Redcross Knight come to Castle Joyous,

Where they were entertaynd with courteous
And comely glee of many gratious
Faire ladies, and of many a gentle knight,
Who through a chamber long and spacious,
Eftsoones them brought unto their ladies sight,
That of them cleeped was the Lady of Delight.
                        (*F. Q.*, III, i, 31.)

In the *De Venus la Deesse d'Amor* the goddess herself
conducts the lover to the court of the God of Love. In the
Romance of the Rose the lover comes to the garden and knocks
upon the door till Ydelnesse, "a mayden curteys," lets him in
and conducts him to the presence of Sir Mirthe, who has with
him

A fair and Ioly companye
Fulfilled of alle curtesye (vv. 639–640).

Here he is met and welcomed by Curtesye herself. We have
already remarked the frequent occurrence of this character in
the love allegories—a fact sufficient in itself to demonstrate
the point made here. In the M. E. *Parliament of Love* the
poet's lady is courteous, gentle, and lowly (vv. 51 ff.).

In the *Romance of the Rose* the lover is admonished by the
God of Love,

Alwey be mery if thou may (v. 2275).

Habitual merriment and gaiety became a recognized obligation
of the courtly aspirant to a lady's favor.[40] In *Astrophel*

---

[40] Cf. Ovid, *Ars amatoria*, II, 175–176; Guillaume de Machaut, *Dit du Vergier*,
Œuvres, ed. by Tarbé, p. 19; Caulier, *L'Hospital d'Amours*, *Œuvres de Chartier*, ed. by
Du Chesne, Paris, 1617, p. 737; and Lydgate, *Temple of Glas*, vv. 1177–1178. Neilson
(*Origins and Sources of the Court of Love*, p. 199) quotes from the Wolfenbüttel MS (15th
Century) the following:
        VII. En toutes compaignies sois et lyes et ioiaus.

Spenser describes Sidney, the courtier and knightly lover, as one who seemed

> made for merriment,
> Merily masking both in bowre and hall:
> There was no pleasure nor delightfull play,
> When Astrophel so ever was away.
>
> (vv. 27–30.)

The Masque of Cupid was ushered in by a "joyous fellowship" of minstrels, "making goodly meriment" (F. Q., III, xii, 5). A number of Spenser's knights appear to be aware of this statute. After overthrowing Sansfoy the Redcross Knight reassured his foe's lady and they rode off together, the knight "feining seemely merth" (F. Q., I, ii, 27). Sir Calidore once came upon a "jolly knight" resting in the shade

> To solace with his lady in delight.
> (F. Q., VI, iii, 20.)

Thus Paridell wooed Hellenore:

> And otherwhyles with amorous delights
> And pleasing toyes he would her entertaine,
> Now singing sweetly, to surprize her sprights,
> Now making layes of love and lovers paine,
> Bransles, ballads, virelayes, and verses vaine;
> Oft purposes, oft riddles he devysed,
> And thousands like, which flowed in his braine,
> With which he fed her fancy, and entysd
> To take to his new love, and leave her old despysd.
>
> (F. Q., III, x, 8.)[41]

In the lovers' paradise described in *An Hymne in Honour of Love* the devotees of the God of Love "feede on nectar heavenly wize,"

> And lie like gods in yvorie beds arayd (v. 285).

They also play

> Their hurtlesse sports, without rebuke or blame (v. 288).

[41] Cf. *Romance of the Rose*, vv. 2317–2328.

When the Redcross Knight and Duessa come to the House of
Pride, the lords and ladies of the court "show off" before them:

> Some frounce their curled heare in courtly guise,
> Some prancke their ruffes, and others trimly dight
> Their gay attyre: each others greater pride does
>   spight (*F. Q.*, I, iv, 14).

The champion of Holiness later quarrels with Sansjoy in the
castle and the combat is appointed for the morrow.   But in the
meantime,

> That night they pas in joy and jollity,
> Feasting and courting both in bowre and hall (St. 43).

In the House of Temperance Lady Alma, having shown the
knights through her palace, brings them back to the parlor:

> And in the midst thereof upon the floure,
> A lovely bevy of faire ladies sate,
> Courted of many a jolly paramoure,
> The which them did in modest wise amate,
> And eachone sought his lady to aggrate:
> And eke emongst them little Cupid playd
> His wanton sportes, being retourned late
> From his fierce warres, and having from him layd
> His cruel bow, wherewith he thousands hath dismayd.
>
> Diverse delights they fownd them selves to please;
> Some song in sweet consort, some laught for joy,
> Some plaid with strawes, some ydly satt at ease;
> But other some could not abide to toy,
> All pleasaunce was to them griefe and annoy:
> This fround, that faund, the third for shame did blush,
> Another seemed envious, or coy,
> Another in her teeth did gnaw a rush:
> But at these straungers presence every one did hush.
>
> Soone as the gracious Alma came in place,
> They all attonce out of their seates arose,
> And to her homage made, with humble grace:
> Whom when the knights beheld, they gan dispose
> Themselves to court, and each a damzell chose.
>   (*F. Q.*, II, ix, 34–36.)

Knight and lady address each other in courtly style—"Gentle
madame" and "Faire sir"—and their conversation consists of

conventional references to love, courtly compliment, and proffers of service.

> Thus they awhile with court and goodly game
> Themselves did solace each one with his dame,
> Till that great lady thence away them sought,
> To vew her castles other wondrous frame.
> (St. 44.)

In the Bower of Bliss two naked maidens sport themselves in the waters of a pool for the delectation of Sir Guyon (*F. Q.,* II, xii, 63–68); and Acrasia and her lover are discovered in amorous embrace (Sts. 72 ff.).[42] In the inner room of Castle Joyous are many beds prepared for ease or delight:

> And all was full of damzels and of squyres,
> Dauncing and reveling both day and night,
> And swimming deepe in sensuall desyres;
> And Cupid still emongst them kindled lustfull fyres.
> (*F. Q.,* III, i, 39.)[43]

Here Britomart and the Redcross Knight are received by Malecasta. All sit down to supper,

> Where they were served with all sumptuous fare,
> Whiles fruitfull Ceres and Lyaeus fatt
> Pourd out their plenty, without spight or spare:
> Nought wanted there that dainty was and rare (St. 51).
>
> . . . .
> Tho were the tables taken all away,
> And every knight and every gentle squire
> Gan choose his dame with *basciomani* gay,
> With whom he ment to make his sport and
> courtly play.
>
> Some fell to daunce, some fel to hazardry,
> Some to make love, some to make meryment,
> As diverse witts to diverse things apply;
> And all the while faire Malecasta bent
> Her crafty engins to her close intent (Sts. 56–57).

In the Garden of Adonis, too, but for Time life would be perfect:

---

[42] These two scenes are, of course, taken from Tasso, *Ger. Lib.,* xv, 58–66 and xvi, 17–26.

[43] Cf. Boccaccio, *La Teseide,* vii, 57.

> For here all plenty and all pleasure flowes,
> And sweete Love gentle fitts amongst them throwes,
> Without fell rancor or fond gealosy:
> Franckly each paramor his leman knowes,
> Each bird his mate, ne any does envy
> Their goodly meriment and gay felicity.
>
> (*F. Q.,* III, vi, 41.)

To this retreat Venus repairs to enjoy in secret the love of Adonis, who lives here in "safe felicity" and sports and plays with Cupid and Psyche (Sts. 49–50). In the House of Busirane is presented the Masque of Cupid with all its attendant revelry (*F. Q.,* III, xii, 3 ff.). Here also the enchanter attempts by the use of magic to compel the love of Amoret (St. 31). Finally, in the garden of the Temple of Venus are shady seats and arbors with convenient walks and alleys:

> And therein thousand payres of lovers walkt,
> Praysing their God, and yeelding him great thankes,
> Ne ever ought but of their true loves talkt,
> Ne ever for rebuke or blame of any balkt.
>
> (*F. Q.,* IV, x, 25.)

Scenes of gaiety and courtly exercise similar in tone and general character to those just described are common in the court of love allegories. Note the following verses from the description of the Court of Fin' Amors in the *Cheltenham MS:*

> E d'autra part ha cent pulsellas,
> Q'anc negus hom non vi plus bellas;
> E chascuna ha son amador,
> E son vestu d'una color,
> Ez baison ez braisson soven,
> E mantenon pretz e joven (vv. 59–64).[44]

In the *Romaunt of the Rose* Idleness gives the lover a history of the garden of Mirth:

> And ofte tyme, him to solace,
> Sir Mirthe cometh into this place,
> And eek with him cometh his meynee,
> That liven in lust and Iolitee (vv. 613–616).

---

[44] Text in *Rev. des Lang. Rom.,* 3rd Ser., vol. VI, 1881, pp. 157 ff.

The lover joins Sir Mirth's company and enjoys the dancing and other forms of merriment:

> The daunces than y-ended were;
> For many of hem that daunced there
> Were with hir loves went awey
> Under the trees to have hir pley.
> A, lord! they lived lustily!
> A gret fool were he, sikerly,
> That nolde, his thankes, swich lyf lede!
> (vv. 1315–1321).

In *La Messe des Oisiaus* of Jean de Condé we have a description of the great company which Venus brings with her to her royal seat:

> Che sambloit uns drois paradis,
> De la joie que demenoient
> Les gens qui avuec li venoient.
> (vv. 68–70.)[45]

Venus has mass sung by the birds and then all sit down to an allegorical feast consisting of "li regars," "dous ris," and a beverage so sweet

> Ke ki le metoit à sa bouche,
> Jà n'en cuidoit avoir son sés (vv. 460–461).

The poet becomes intoxicated. Then sighs and complaints are served. After a while the waiters bring out for the ladies a course

> De biaus respons, de dous otrois (v. 522).

From a beautiful maiden the poet receives one of the first but is refused the second. Then there is more excessive drinking:

> Après servirent li servant
> D'un més pour lecheurs apaisier:
> Acoler furent et baisier,
> De coi mains amans tant avoit
> Com il demander en savoit (vv. 598–602).

---

[45] *Dits et Contes*, ed. by Scheler, Brussels, 1867, vol. 3, p. 3.

After the feast Venus hears those who have complaints.   In Hawes' *Pastime of Pleasure* the lover slays a three-headed giant and is met by three ladies—Verity, Good Operation, and Fidelity—who conduct him to their castle, salve his wounds, and set him down to a good supper prepared by Temperance. During the meal he tells them of La Belle Pucell and of his desire to win her.   They commend his zeal and wish him success:

> Thus did we passe time in all maner of joye,
> I lacketh nothyng that might make me solace,
> But evermore, as noble Troyelus of Troy,
> Full ofte I thought on my fayre ladyes face,
> And her to se a muche longer space.
> When time was come, to rest I was brought,
> All to me longyng there lacked right nought.[46]

The joy and gaiety of the court of love find expression also in harp and voice.   Music in various forms pervades the atmosphere.   On the morn of his combat with the Pagan the Redcross Knight rises early and comes into the great "commune hall" of the House of Pride:

> There many minstrales maken melody,
> To drive away the dull melancholy,
> And many bardes, that to the trembling chord
> Can tune their timely voices cunningly,
> And many chroniclers, that can record
> Old loves, and warres for ladies doen by
>   many a lord (*F. Q.,* I, v, 3).

So also in the Bower of Bliss, as Sir Guyon and the palmer approach the hidden retreat of Acrasia,

> Eftsoones they heard a most melodious sound,
> Of all that mote delight a daintie eare,
> Such as attonce might not on living ground
> Save in this paradise, be heard elswhere:
> Right hard it was for wight which did it heare,
> To read what manner musicke that mote bee:
> For all that pleasing is to living eare
> Was there consorted in one harmonee;
> Birdes, voices, instruments, windes, waters,
>   all agree.

[46] *Percy Soc.,* vol. 18, p. 169.

> The joyous birdes, shrouded in chearefull shade,
> Their notes unto the voice attempred sweet:
> Th' angelicall soft trembling voyces made
> To th' instruments divine respondence meet:
> The silver sounding instruments did meet
> With the base murmure of the waters fall:
> The waters fall with difference discreet,
> Now soft, now loud, unto the wind did call:
> The gentle warbling wind low answered to all.
> <div align="right">(<i>F. Q.</i>, II, xii, 70 and 71.)</div>

They find the witch and her lover resting in a secret shade:

> Whilst round about them pleasauntly did sing
> Many faire ladies and lascivious boyes,
> That ever mixt their song with light
>   licentious toyes (St. 72).

Moreover, the great chamber of Castle Joyous is filled with revelers:

> And all the while sweet music did divide
> Her looser notes with Lydian harmony.
> <div align="right">(<i>F. Q.</i>, III, i, 40.)</div>

Parallels are not far to seek. Music is given prominence in the festivities of Sir Mirth's court in the *Romaunt of the Rose*:

> Tho mightest thou caroles seen,
> And folk ther daunce and mery been,
> And make many a fair tourning
> Upon the grene gras springing.
> Ther mightest thou see these floutours,
> Minstrales, and eek Iogelours,
> That wel to singe dide hir peyne.
> (vv. 759–765.)

Compare the court of Venus in Jean de Condé's *La Messe des Oisiaus*:

> iiii menestreil de vïele
> Ont une estampie nouviele
> Devant la dame vïelée.
> Là fu joie renouvelée:
> Maint menestreil de cuer entier
> Y servirent de lor mestier (vv. 641–646).

In the *Hous of Fame* Chaucer describes the castle of the goddess as full

> Of alle maner of minstrales,
> And gestiours, that tellen tales
> Bothe of weping and of game,
> Of al that longeth unto Fame (vv. 1197–1200).

He heard Orpheus and many other famous musicians playing, and others that "maden loude menstralcyes" (v. 1217) upon all manner of pipes, flutes, and horns.

Special hymns of complaint, prayer, or praise form a part of the service due the presiding deity in the court of love. These hymns are often of an ecclesiastical or classico-religious flavor.   To such a composition Spenser doubtless alludes in *An Hymne in Honour of Love,* where the poet expresses an earnest longing to join the happy company in the paradise of the God of Love:

> Then would I sing of thine immortall praise
> An heavenly hymne, such as the angels sing,
> And thy triumphant name then would I raise
> Bove all the gods, thee onely honoring,
> My guide, my god, my victor, and my king:
> Till then, dread lord, vouchsafe to take of me
> This simple song, thus fram'd in praise of thee.
>   (vv. 301–307.)

Indeed, the whole poem is itself in form and spirit such a hymn, as the last two lines quoted above indicate.   The typical example in Spenser, however, is the hymn to Venus sung by a lover in the temple of the goddess (*F. Q.,* IV, x, 44–47).[47] The lover's hymn is sung amid surroundings characteristic of the court of love environment:

> And all about her altar, scattered lay
> Great sorts of lovers piteously complayning,
> Some of their losse, some of their loves delay,
> Some of their pride, some paragons disdayning,

---

[47] In the Bower of Bliss we have a song on the "Carpe diem" theme—dear to Elizabethans—which Spenser translated from Tasso, but which, while perfectly appropriate to the setting, is not strictly of the type under discussion. Cf. *F. Q.,* II, xii, 74–75 and *Ger. Lib.,* xvi, 14–15.

> Some fearing fraud, some fraudulently fayning,
> As every one had cause of good or ill.
>
> > (*F. Q.,* IV, x, 43.)

Compare with this the scene in the M. E. *Court of Love,* where the author and other lovers enter the temple and see the golden image of Venus:

> And there we founde a thousand on their knee,
> Sum freshe and feire, som dedely to behold,
> In sondry mantils new, and som were old,
> Som painted were with flames rede as fire,
> Outward to shew their inward hoot desire.
>
> > (vv.   570–574.)

Some of these cried to Venus for mercy and for vengeance on the "false untrew;" and others, "a thousand milion," rejoiced and sang praise to the goddess.[48]   Constrained by the irresistible power of love Spenser's lover breaks out into a paean of praise, setting forth the power of Venus over all animate nature—over storm and cloud, over budding flower and singing bird, over the beast of the field, and over every source of joy and beauty, and closing with the brief but fervent appeal:

> O graunt that of my love at last I may not misse.

As is well known, Spenser in this hymn has paraphrased the invocation to Venus found at the beginning of the *De Rerum Natura.*[49]   In so doing Spenser may have had in mind the example of his master, Chaucer, who uses the same theme—the power of Venus or Love over all animate nature—but in a more condensed form, in the invocation to the Goddess of Love which

---

[48] Cf. references cited by Schick in the introduction to his edition of Lydgate's *Temple of Glas,* E. E. T. S., 1891, p. cxx (footnote).

[49] Sawtelle, *The Sources of Spenser's Classical Mythology,* p. 119.

forms the proem to the third book of *Troilus and Criseyde*.[50]
A similar idea is set forth in the hymn of praise sung by the
happy lovers who throng the temple of Venus in the M. E.
Court of Love.[51]   Just as in the latter poem the lovers' hymn
is followed by the author's own plea, so in Spenser the anony-
mous lover's song is followed by Scudamour's brief petition:

> So did he say: but I with murmure soft,
> That none might heare the sorrow of my hart,
> Yet inly groning deepe and sighing oft,
> Besought her to graunt ease unto my smart,
> And to my wound her gratious help impart.
>
> (*F. Q.*, IV, x, 48.)

Overcoming the opposition of Womanhood the knightly lover
presses his suit for the love of Amoret, as he hopes for a favorable response to his prayer:

> And evermore upon the goddesse face
> Mine eye was fixt, for feare of her offence:
> Whom when I saw with amiable grace
> To laugh at me, and favour my pretence,
> I was emboldned with more confidence,
> And nought for nicenesse nor for envy sparing,
> In presence of them all forth led her thence,
> All looking on, and like astonish staring,
> Yet to lay hand on her not one of all them daring.
>
> (St. 56.)

In Lydgate's *Temple of Glas* the lover enters an oratory of
Venus and prays for help for his mortal woe:

[50] O blisful light, of whiche the bemes clere
Adorneth al the thridde hevene faire!
O sonnes leef, O Ioves doughter dere,
Plesaunce of love, O goodly debonaire,
In gentil hertes ay redy to repaire!
O verray cause of hele and of gladnesse,
Y-heried by thy might and thy goodnesse!

In hevene and helle, in erthe and salte see
Is felt thy might, if that I wel descerne;
As man, brid, best, fish, herbe and grene tree
Thee fele in tymes with vapour eterne.
God loveth, and to love wol nought werne;
And in this world no lyves creature,
With-outen love, is worth, or may endure (vv. 1–14).

[51] Cf., for example, the following lines:
Venus, redresse of all division,
Goddess eterne, thy name y-heried is!
By loves bond is knit all thing, y-wis,
Best unto best, the erth to water wan,
Bird unto bird, and woman unto man;

This is the lyfe of joye that we ben in,
Resembling lyfe of hevenly paradyse (vv. 591–597).

> And þouȝ so be I can not wele expresse
> The grevous harmes þat I fele in myn hert,
> Haveþ never þe les merci of my smert.
>   (vv. 712–714.)

Venus favors his suit:

> And þerwithal Venus, as me þouȝt,
> Toward þis man ful benygneli
> Gan cast hir eyȝe, liche as þouȝ she rouȝt
> Of his disease (vv. 848–851).

Emboldened by the goddess' favor and promise of aid the lover goes to his lady and makes his plea for mercy. The lady is visibly confused and perturbed through maidenly fear, for

> Hir bloode astonyed so from her herte ran
> Into hir face, of femynynite:
> Thuruȝ honest drede abaisshed so was she.
>   (vv. 1044–1046.)

Amoret is also timid and reluctant:

> She often prayd, and often me besought,
> Sometime with tender teares to let her goe,
> Sometime with witching smyles: but yet, for
>   nought
> That ever she to me could say or doe,
> Could she her wished freedome fro me wooe.
>   (F. Q., IV, x, 57.)

Likewise, in Lydgate's poem the lady finally yields to the will of Venus and the importunity of her lover, and they are united by the goddess.[52]

The birds also contribute their part to the joyous music of the court of love. Their songs are in harmony with the environment, for they always sing of love. Thus the birds are endowed with a certain intelligence that enables them to enter sympathetically into the lovers' songs of joy or despair.

---

[52] Instances of this kind, where Venus intervenes on behalf of the lover, are too common in the court of love poems to call for special comment. In the *Romaunt of the Rose* (vv. 3726 ff.) the goddess remonstrates with Bel-Acueil, declaring that the lover deserves to kiss the rose as Love's servant and as the embodiment of all the courtly virtues.

In the Bower of Bliss they join with voices, instruments, winds, and waters to produce a pleasing harmony (*F. Q.*, II, xii, 70).[53] In the same scene some one sings a lay urging lovers to

> Gather the rose of love, whilest yet is time (St. 75).

> He ceast, and then gan all the quire of birdes
> Their diverse notes t'attune unto his lay,
> As in approvaunce of his pleasing wordes (St. 76).[54]

In Castle Joyous there is a continual sound of music:

> And all the while sweet birdes thereto applide
> Their daintie layes and dulcet melody,
> Ay caroling of love and jollity,
> That wonder was to heare their trim consort.
>   (*F. Q.*, III, i, 40.)

In the Garden of Adonis flowers and fruits flourish in a perpetual spring:

> The whiles the joyous birdes make their pastyme
> Emongst the shady leaves, their sweet abode,
> And their trew loves without suspition tell abrode.
>   (*F. Q.*, III, vi, 42.)

In the *De Nuptiis* Venus is so careful of the songs of her birds that she admits none who can not pass a voice test.[55] Compare also with Spenser the *De Venus la Deesse d'Amor*:

> Des oiseillons i ot plus de mil cens,
> Cascun cantoit d'amors selonc son sens (7).

In the *Romaunt of the Rose* the lover approaches the garden and hears the songs of the birds,

> whiche thereinne were,
> That songen, through hir mery throtes,
> Daunces of love, and mery notes (vv. 506–508).[56]

---

[53] Cf. Chaucer, *Parlement of Foules*, vv. 190–203.

[54] These passages are taken from Tasso, *Ger. Lib.*, xvi, 12–16; but note that the lay of love, sung in Tasso by a bird, is by Spenser put into the mouth of a person.

[55] Umbrosumque nemus, quo non admittitur ales,
Ni probet ante suos Diva sub judice cantus.
Quae placuit, fruitur ramis: quae victa, recedit.
                         (vv. 62–64.)

[56] See also vv. 655–684.

So also in the Cheltenham court of love *MS*:

> E d'autra part hac un ombrage,
> On hac maint bel auzel saulvatge,
> Que canton la nueit e lo zor
> Voltas e lais de gran dousor (vv. 67–70).[57]

Other miscellaneous references in Spenser connect the birds with lovers and their songs. In the June eclogue of the *Shepheardes Calender* Hobbinol says to Colin that the echo of his "rymes and roundelayes" taught the birds to

> Frame to thy songe their cheerful cheriping,
> Or hold theyr peace, for shame of thy swete layes.
>   (vv. 55–56.)

In the August eclogue Cuddie sings Colin's plaint:

> Ye carelesse byrds are privie to my cryes,
> Which in your songs were wont to make
>   a part (vv. 153–154).[58]

In *Daphnaida* the bereaved lover says:

> But I will wake and sorrow all the night
> With Philumene, my fortune to deplore,
> With Philumene, the partner of my plight.
>   (vv. 474–476.)

In the forest glade where Belphoebe dwells are myrtle and laurel trees,

> In which the birds song many a lovely lay
> Of Gods high praise, and of their loves sweet teene,
> As it an earthly paradize had beene.
>   (*F. Q.*, III, v, 40.)

After Belphoebe and her squire have been estranged through jealousy, a dove comes to condole with the lover and finally brings the lady to him, thus effecting a reconciliation.[59]

---

[57] *Rev. des Lang. Rom.*, 3rd Ser., VI, 1881, p. 159. Cf. also Deschamps, *Le Lay Amoureux*, vv. 9–14; Guillaume de Machaut, *Dit du Vergier, Œuvres*, ed. by Tarbé, p. 12; and the *De Phillide et Flora*, vv. 249–256.

[58] Cf. also vv. 183–186.

[59] In *Li Romanz de la Poire* the God of Love sends a nightingale to accompany the lover to his lady (vv. 2928 ff.). Text ed. by F. Stehlich, Halle, 1881, pp. 111 ff.

Although Spenser makes the birds and their songs a part of the court of love setting, he does not employ a choir of birds to sing a parody of the church service in honor and laudation of a love deity, typical examples of which are found in *La Messe des Oisiaus* (vv. 113 ff.) of Jean de Condé and in the M. E. *Court of Love* (vv. 1352 ff.). There are two passages in his work, however, which seem to be direct references to the birds' parodies and which show that the convention left a distinct impression on his mind. In *Amoretti* 19 he says:

> The merry cuckow, messenger of Spring,
> His trompet shrill hath thrise already sounded,
> That warnes al lovers wayt upon their king,
> Who now is coming forth with girland crouned.
> With noyse whereof the quyre of byrds resounded
> Their anthemes sweet, devized of Loves prayse,
> That all the woods theyr ecchoes back rebounded,
> As if they knew the meaning of their layes.

In *La Messe des Oisiaus* the *papegai* comes to warn the birds to be prepared to wait upon Venus at her approach and to make "tel joie qu'il convient" (v. 43). The cuckoo holds a less dignified position, for it is he who interrupts the service held in honor of Venus and has to be chased out (vv. 300 ff.). Note that Spenser speaks of a "quyre" of birds and that they sing "anthemes" in praise of the God of Love as he comes in triumph. The second passage is in the *Epithalamion*. The poet hails the dawn of his wedding day:

> Hark how the cheerefull birds do chaunt theyr laies,
> And carroll of loves praise!
> The merry larke hir mattins sings aloft,
> The thrush replyes, the mavis descant playes,
> The ouzell shrills, the ruddock warbles soft,
> So goodly all agree, with sweet consent,
> To this dayes merriment (vv. 78–84).[60]

With this compare the M. E. *Court of Love*:

---

[60] Cf. Heywood's "Pack, clouds, away," from *The Repe of Lucrece*, Act IV, Sc. vi (Mermaid Series, p. 396). For this and other Elizabethan parallels I am indebted to Prof. A. H. Tolman.

Cf. also Spenser's refrain and its echo in Amoretti XIX. For this parallel I am indebted to Mr. Percy W. Long.

On May-day, whan the lark began to ryse,
To matens went the lusty nightingale
Within a temple shapen hawthorn-wise.
(vv. 1352–1354.)

The "thrustell-cok," the mavis, and the robin are among the birds which take part in the service sung in praise of the Lord of Love.

In his treatise on the art of love Andreas Capellanus sets forth a series of rules apparently designed to govern the intimate relations of lover and mistress. One of these laws requires of both lover and lady a due observance of modesty.[61] The principle here laid down was faithfully kept by Spenser's honorable knights and ladies in their courtly intercourse.

Arriving at the Castle of Medina Sir Guyon was led up into a bower by the lady of the castle in person,

And comely courted with meet modestie.
(F. Q., II, ii, 15.)

Sir Artegall was careful in his wooing of Britomart:

Besides her modest countenance he saw
So goodly grave, and full of princely aw,
That it his ranging fancie did refraine,
And looser thoughts to lawfull bounds
withdraw (F. Q., IV, vi, 33).

Marinell was joyful at sight of Florimell,

Ne lesse was she in secret hart affected,
But that she masked it with modestie,
For feare she should of lightnesse be
detected (F. Q., IV, xii, 35).

In contrast to this regard for modesty stands out the conduct of certain of the poet's unworthy characters. It was the unmaidenly conduct of the false image of Una, sent to the Redcross Knight's couch by Archimago, that so astonished the Champion of Holiness and made him suspect her truth (F. Q.,

---

[61] In amoris praestando et recipiendo solatia omnis debet verecundiae pudor adesse.
(De Amore, ed. by Trojel, p. 106.)

I, i, 53). The law was boldly violated by the unknightly
Cymochles and the loose maidens in the Bower of Bliss (*F. Q.,*
II, v, 32–34). Sir Guyon had the misfortune to fall in with
one of these followers of Acrasia:

> The knight was courteous, and did not forbeare
> Her honest merth and pleasuance to partake;
> But when he saw her toy, and gibe, and geare,
> And passe the bonds of modest merimake,
> Her dalliaunce he despisd, and follies did
>   forsake (*F. Q.,* II, vi, 21).

In like manner Malecasta overstepped the bounds of modesty
in her unbridled overtures to Britomart whose sex she mistook
(*F. Q.,* III, i, 48).[62]

Spenser's standard of courtly conduct agrees with the code
of Andreas Capellanus in yet another point. The latter enun-
ciates certain statutes against meddling, one of which states that
no one should attempt to break up a legitimate love affair.[63]
In the June eclogue of the *Shepheardes Calender* Colin longs
for poetic power to enable him to be revenged on a meddling
rival:

> And thou, Menalcas, that by trechere
> Didst underfong my lasse to wexe so light,
> Shouldest well be knowne for such
>   thy villanee (vv. 102–104).

In *Epithalamion* the poet bids night wrap him and his love in
its mantle and keep them from peril:

> Let no false treason seeke us to entrap,
> Nor any dread disquiet once annoy
> The safety of our joy (vv. 323–325).

Andreas Capellanus also warns lovers against lying, tale-
bearing, and slander.[64] Fear and hatred of scandal-mongers

---

[62] Modesty, it should be remembered, is one of the damsels in attendance in the Temple
of Venus (*F. Q.,* IV, x, 51.)

[63] Alterius idonee copulatam amori scienter subvertere non coneris.
(*De Amore,* ed. by Trojel, p. 106.)

[64] Mendacia omnino vitare memento.
Maledicus esse non debes.
Amantium noli exsistere propalator.
(*De Amore,* ed. by Trojel, p. 106.)

In the *Romance of the Rose* we are told that the trouble which arose when the lover
kissed the rose was due to
Wikked tunge that fals espie
Which is so glad to feyne and lye (vv. 3871–3872).

are quite commonly voiced in mediaeval courtly poetry.[65] It was they who furnished the chief motive to secrecy.[66]

Similarly in Spenser we find a cordial dislike of tattlers in courtly society. In *Amoretti* 85 the poet calls up all the plagues and pains of hell against the "venemous toung,"

> That with false forged lyes, which thou didst tel,
> In my true love did stirre up coles of yre.

In *Epithalamion* the poet says:

> Ne let false whispers, breeding hidden feares,
> Breake gentle sleepe with misconceived dout.
> (vv. 336–337.)

Among the woes of the lover recounted in *An Hymne in Honour of Love* are

> The false reports that flying tales doe beare (v. 261).

In *Mother Hubberds Tale* Spenser says that while the common courtier likes "to gybe and fleare at everie thing, which they heare spoken ill," the honorable courtier

> Doth loath such base condition, to backbite
> Anies good name for envie or despite.
> (vv. 719–720.)[67]

In the House of Temperance the porter kept watch day and night:

> Utterers of secrets he from thence debard,
> Bablers of folly, and blazers of crime.
> (*F. Q.*, II, ix, 25.)

---

[65] For example, Bernart de Ventadorn thus vents his bitter enmity:
> Ai Dieus! car si fosson trian
> d'entrels fals li fin amador,
> e·l lauzengier e·l trichador
> portesson corns el fron denan!
> (Appel, *Prov. Chrest.*, p. 56.)

[66] In the M. E. *Court of Love* lovers are admonished to be secret,
> Exyling slaunder ay for dred and fere (v. 313).

[67] Cf. Gower (*Confessio Amantis*, II, 449–451):
> Bot yit fulofte it is believed,
> And many a worthie love is grieved
> Thurgh bacbitinge of fals Envie.

Spenser's natural repugnance to slander led him to an allegorical representation of its hideousness in two separate instances. First, it is an old hag who lives in a lonely cottage and vents her spleen on the chance visitor forced by circumstances to find shelter beneath her roof:

> Ne ever knight so bold, ne ever dame
> So chast and loyall liv'd, but she would strive
> With forged cause them falsely to defame.
> (*F. Q.*, IV, viii, 25.)[68]

An even more pretentious personification of this social scourge is given in the Blatant Beast, a monster sent forth from Stygian den,

> To be the plague and scourge of wretched men:
> Whom with vile tongue and venemous intent
> He sore doth wound, and bite, and cruelly
> torment (*F. Q.*, VI, i, 8).

He lured Timias into ambush and wounded both the squire and the lady Serena:

> Ne ever knight, that bore so lofty creast,
> Ne ever lady of so honest name,
> But he them spotted with reproch, or
> secrete shame (*F. Q.*, VI, vi, 12).

The hermit at whose cell the wounded lady and the injured squire stopped to recuperate gave them some advice as to how they might avoid the hurts of the Beast:

> Abstaine from pleasure, and restraine your will,
> Subdue desire, and bridle loose delight,
> Use scanted diet, and forbeare your fill,
> Shun secresie, and talke in open sight:
> So shall you soone repaire your present
> evill plight (*F. Q.*, VI, vi, 14).

Sir Calidore finally overtook and overcame the monster. He clapped an iron muzzle over the mouth of the Beast,

> And therein shut up his blasphemous tong,
> For never more defaming gentle knight,
> Or unto lovely lady doing wrong.[69]
> (*F. Q.*, VI, xii, 34.)

---

[68] Cf. Godfrey Gobilyve, or *False Reporte*, in Hawes, *Pastime of Pleasure*, Percy Soc. Pub., vol. XVIII, pp. 134 ff.
[69] Cf. the injunction in the *Romance of the Rose*:
> And if that ony myssaiere
> Dispise wymmen that thou maist here
> Blame hym and bidde hym holde hym stille.
> (vv. 2231–2233.)

SPENSER'S OVIDIAN LOVER

In an article on the unity of the third book of the *Faerie Queene* Professor Padelford has drawn sharp attention to the Paridell-Hellenore episode of the ninth and tenth cantos in the unqualified statement that this story is "the most dramatic and realistic tale of the whole *Faerie Queene.*"[1] This is strong language, but there are good reasons for it. The scholar just quoted has indicated some of these; I wish to point out one or two others. The dramatic and realistic qualities noted, together with an unwonted vein of sardonic humor which pervades these scenes, are partly due in my opinion to Spenser's use of Ovid or the traditional Ovidian code in the details of Paridell's wooing and winning of Hellenore.

First of all, let us recall in outline the story of cantos nine and ten. A company of knights including Paridell (who had left court to rescue the lost Florimell), Satyrane, the Squire of Dames, and Britomart arrives at the castle of Malbecco and finds the gates shut against them. The adventurers force entrance and receive a cold welcome. They sit down to supper but refuse to eat till the lady of the castle appears to grace the board. The old, half-blind, miserly, and jealous husband reluctantly yields, and the young wife joins the company. During the meal the accomplished lover Paridell, seated on Malbecco's blind side, plies the seducer's art so successfully that the ill-mated wife lends a favorable ear. Early next morning the other guests ride away, but Paridell lingers and, having completed his conquest, elopes with Hellenore. Old Malbecco pursues but is halted and robbed; and when he finally overtakes his wife in the forest, she has already been deserted by her lover and is now living in contentment as the common property of the satyrs. She refuses to return home, and the old husband in rage and despair throws himself from a rock into the sea, but is so wasted that he falls lightly and is caught by his "crooked clawes" on a cliff, from which he

---

[1] *Studies in Philology*, XXI, 1924, 379.

manages to crawl into a cave, where he still lives on with "todes and frogs," but

> "Is woxen so deform'd, that he has quight
> Forgot he was a man, and Gelosy is hight."
>
> (F. Q., III, x, 60.)

So much for the episode as a whole. Now let us note somewhat more in detail the conduct of Paridell and Hellenore in the wooing scenes. The intrigue begins at the dinner in Malbecco's castle. Here we have a typically Ovidian setting.[2] Given a jealous husband with a handsome wife, the gay lover's chief ambition in life is to outwit the husband, against whom lover and mistress are now pitted in the game of love. In playing this game the eyes must be used to convey secret messages. Seated on Malbecco's blind side Paridell is able to do this unobserved:

> On her faire face so did he feede his fill,
> And sent close messages of love to her at will.
>
> And ever and anone, when none was ware,
> With speaking lookes, that close embassage bore,
> He rov'd at her and told his secret care:
> For all that art he learned had of yore.
> Ne was she ignoraunt of that leud lore,
> But in his eye his meaning wisely redd,
> And with the like him aunswered evermore.
>
> (F. Q., III, ix, 27–28.)

In like manner Ovid instructs his mistress how to act at the banquet which her husband is also to attend:

> Me specta nutusque meos vultumque loquacem;
>   excipe furtivas et refer ipsa notas.
> Verba superciliis sine voce loquentia dicam.
>
> (Amores, I, iv, 17–19.)

Paridell also makes use of wine to convey his secret love:

> Now Bacchus fruit out of the silver plate
> He on the table dasht, as overthrowne,
> Or of the fruitfull liquor overflowne,

[2] Cf. Amores, I, iv.

> And by the dauncing bubbles did divine,
> Or therein write to lett his love be showne.
>
> (*F. Q.*, III, ix, 30.)

So in Ovid:

> Verba leges digitis, verba notata mero.
>
> (*Amores*, I, iv, 20.)

Hellenore makes a further use of wine as a part of the sign language:

> And when so of his hand the pledge she raught,
> The guilty cup she fained to mistake,
> And in her lap did shed her idle draught,
> Shewing desire her inward flame to slake.
>
> (*F. Q.*, III, ix, 31.)[3]

Paridell thus shows himself a complete master of the art of love-making:

> So perfect in that art was Paridell,
> That he Malbeccoes halfen eye did wyle.
>
> (*F. Q.*, III, x, 5.)

In the courtly system love-making is conceived of as an art— a science to be mastered. This view is primarily Ovidian:[4]

> Si quis in hoc artem populo non novit amandi,
> Me legat; et lecto carmine doctus amet.
> Arte citae veloque rates remoque moventur:
> Arte leves currus, arte regendus Amor.
>
> (*Ars am.*, I, 1–4.)

With the Latin poet the art consists in a politic regulation of conduct towards the mistress with the practical aim of seduction. Robbed of sentiment, love becomes a matter of cold-blooded calculation. Art is reduced to artifice.

---

[3] For other, though less striking, parallels compare *F. Q.*, III, x, 6 with *Ars amatoria*, I, 143–144, and *F. Q.*, III, x, 8 with *Ars amatoria*, I, 595–596. That Paridell's love-making is purely a matter of artifice appears from *F. Q.*, III, x, 7. On the general subject of Spenser's indebtedness to Ovid, see Riedner, *Spenser's Belesenheit*, Leipzig, 1908, pp. 105 ff.

[4] See Schrötter, W., *Ovid und die Troubadours*, Halle, 1908, pp. 95 ff.

Ovid, for example, instructs his lover in the art of sighing and weeping:

> et lacrimae prosunt: lacrimis adamanta movebis.
> fac madidas videat, si potes, illa genas.[5]

Paridell, in paying court to Hellenore, follows a similar method:

> He sigh'd, he sobd, he swownd, he perdy dyde. . .
> He wept, and wayld, and false laments belyde.
> (F. Q., III, x, 7.)

In a final appeal, he declares that, in default of her favor, "he mote algates dye, yet did his death forgive." As Schrötter remarks, the protestation that one is dying of longing is prescribed by Ovid and is regarded by him as well as by the troubadours as the expression of highest, boundless love.[6]

Recognizing, however, the value of versatility in the art of love, Ovid likewise instructs the lover to cultivate the opposite virtue of merriment and gaiety in the presence of the mistress.

> Proelia sum Parthis, cum culta pax sit amica
> et iocus, et causas quicquid amoris habet.[7]

Thus also Paridell woos Hellenore:

> And otherwhyles with amorous delights
> And pleasing toyes he would her entertaine,
> Now singing sweetly, to surprize her sprights,
> Now making layes of love and lovers paine,
> Bransles, ballads, virelayes, and verses vaine.
> (F. Q., III, x, 8.)

These parallels strengthen the conviction that, though Paridell may be, as he boasts, nominally descended from Paris, he has received his courtly education either directly from Ovid

---

[5] *Ars am.*, I, 657–660. Cf. *ibid*, III, 675–676.
[6] *Ovid und die Troubadours*, p. 76.
[7] *Ars am.*, II, 175–176.

or from the Ovidian tradition, which may be said to have persisted as the conventional basis of the system of courtly love even after the philosophy of love had been completely transformed by Renaissance Platonism.   It matters little for the present purpose whether Spenser's debt to Ovid be direct or indirect. The arresting fact is that the "sage and serious" Spenser, though permeated from his Cambridge days with the Neo-Platonic philosophy of love, creates a typically Ovidian lover, endows him with the social equipment and callous philosophy of the breed, and then conducts him to a triumphant conclusion of his lawless quest. Why does he do this? The answer to the question is found in the purpose of the poet in this episode to portray, in the words of Professor Padelford, "the disastrous consequences to chastity when youthful charm and spirit are wedded to jealous old age."[8] Not that Spenser disliked the seducer less, but that for the time being he hated the jealous dotard more. In the Ovidian lover the poet finds a fit means for venting his scorn and contempt of old Malbecco, the real enemy of marital chastity. Out of the situation thus created grows naturally the dramatic realism, the pungent humor and the biting satire already alluded to. The creation of Paridell was a stroke of art.

[8] *Studies in Philology,* April, 1924, p. 379.

CONCLUSION

A detailed analysis of Spenser's poetry and a comparison of obvious courtly love conventions found there with the same commonplaces in mediaeval courtly literature show that both in his shorter lyrics, where he speaks in his own person as a courtly poet, and in the *Faerie Queene,* where his worthy knights scrupulously follow the code of chivalric love, Spenser consistently adheres to the recognized customs, usages, and laws of the courtly system.

However, the sage and serious laureate of the ideal gentleman, the creator of Sir Calidore and the author of the *Fowre Hymnes,* whom Milton dared to think a better teacher than Aquinas, utterly rejects the ethical and moral implications of the traditional code and upholds an ideal love philosophy compounded of Puritan and Platonic elements. For him true love is always chaste and quite compatible with marriage. Although as an artist he may avail himself of the courtly conceits, in *Colin Clouts Come Home Againe* he distinctly separates himself from the "vaine votaries of laesie love" who infested the court on his return in 1589 and abused the high calling of the courtly poet. Likewise in the *Amoretti* he is careful to state that the Beauty he worships in his lady is Platonic and that her love

> "Not like to lusts of baser kynd,
> The harder wonne, the firmer will abide."
> (Sonnet 6.)

Again, in Sonnet 83, he prays that no spark of "filthy lustfull fyre" nor no glance of "sensuall desyre" may break out in him to annoy his lady. There can, therefore, be little doubt that, as between the Ovidian and the Platonic philosophies of love, Spenser personally embraced the latter and adhered to it to the end of his career.

01